THE
ORESTEIA

THE
ORESTEIA
by
AESCHYLUS

A new translation for the theater by
David Grene and
Wendy Doniger O'Flaherty

With introductions by
David Grene, Wendy Doniger O'Flaherty,
and Nicholas Rudall

The University of Chicago Press
Chicago and London

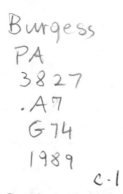

DAVID GRENE is professor in the Committee on Social Thought at the University of Chicago. WENDY DONIGER O'FLAHERTY is the Mircea Eliade Professor in the Divinity School at the University of Chicago. NICHOLAS RUDALL is associate professor of classical language and literature at the University of Chicago and artistic director of the Court Theater.

The University of Chicago Press, Chicago 60637
The University of Chicago Press, Ltd., London

© 1989 by The University of Chicago
All rights reserved. Published 1989
Printed in the United States of America

98 97 96 95 94 93 92 91 90 89   54321

Library of Congress Cataloging in Publication Data

Aeschylus.
    [Oresteia. English]
    The Oresteia / by Aeschylus : a new translation for the theater by
David Grene and Wendy Doniger O'Flaherty : with introductions by
David Grene, Wendy Doniger O'Flaherty, and Nicholas Rudall.
        p.   cm.
    ISBN 0-226-00771-5.   ISBN 0-226-00772-3 (pbk.)
    1. Orestes (Greek mythology)—Drama.   I. Grene, David.
II. O'Flaherty, Wendy Doniger.   III. Title.
PA3827.A7G74 1989
882'.01—dc19   88-20492
                                                                     CIP

To David Tracy
with love and admiration
for all that his participation in the *Oresteia* seminar
meant for us,
the translators

CONTENTS

NOTE

In the Chicago series there is already a translation of the *Oresteia*, all three plays of it rendered by the same author, Richmond Lattimore. This version now before you is in no sense intended to supersede the other. Lattimore's rendering of the *Oresteia* has been widely and justly acclaimed as one of the outstanding twentieth-century recreations of the play in verse. Connected as I was with the beginning of the Chicago series, and seeing Lattimore's *Oresteia* as one of its best efforts, the last thing I would want to do—even were it possible—is to supersede it.

This *Oresteia* of ours has a different purpose from his. Wendy O'Flaherty and I set out to write an *Oresteia* that was entirely speakable by a modern actor in English, on a modern stage—and Nick Rudall wanted to make his stage play out of as much of our translation as he thought the needs of his theater could accommodate. The cutting edge of our assignment was the necessity to convey this Greek play in a medium where the words spoken by a modern actor would carry instant conviction.

Very clearly, with the two collaborators I had, this could not be done at the expense of the truth of the translation from the Greek into English. But the truth of a translation has different colors. There is a color which harmonizes with the reader in his study, and perhaps with the teacher in his class. Such a translation permits of a constant interruption by the reader's second thoughts ("That expression does not sound like the Greek to me," if the reader knows Greek, or "I wonder what that means," as the mind grapples again with the words, as they begin to haunt our imaginations and their first immediate impression is lost). Or the reading of a teacher may be interrupted by himself saying,

"There is another significance that is possible in this passage, and it is this. . . ."

But our job is different. First of all, the words spoken on the stage do not admit of any such corrections. Their meaning must be transparent, overwhelming, and must be able to reach the audience through the histrionic voice and movements of the actor. They must also be ongoing; that is, all the words in a passage give a meaning charged with implications for the character of the man in the play—and especially in the *Oresteia* with meaning for the character of the two women in the play, Clytemnestra and Cassandra. The translator's work in furnishing the actors with these words is a neck-or-nothing venture. He is committed to one meaning because his audience's reception of the passage occurs at one time and without correction or interruption. I know that several times in this version we were compelled to choose one meaning and neglect another, almost equally likely to be correct. We must then stick by the implications of how we had rendered this passage for the rest of the play. We did not do so, or I hope extremely rarely, because we mistook the meaning of the Greek or cut our losses by choosing an easier solution over a harder one.

This is, honestly, not a less literal version than Lattimore's, but his is a translation that can afford to be equivocal; he is appealing from an immediate effect to a rereading, or to a teacher who can afford to insist on his students' recognizing an ambiguity. No actor, as he speaks, dare leave his audience in doubt as to what he is saying—unless he is obviously calling our attention to his doing just that.

Why then print this version for reading at all? Why not let it rest in the theatrical performance? I think that the justification for printing this, in a form we thought was completely sayable in its entirety, or in Rudall's cut version, which we know was sayable and very effective as such because it was played before large audiences for many weeks, is that the *Oresteia* was written to be spoken on the stage. Acting is as integral to its meaning, in its sharpest and most definite form, as color is to van Gogh's painting. Of course, the Greek theater is different in many ways from ours. Undoubtedly, we make many mistakes about how these plays affected their audience. But the essential quality which unites all acting is there—there is a body and a voice on the stage speaking directly, and not so directly, to people assembled to listen, and moved with the emotion and passions that the voice and the body induce us to participate in. Also, the Greek *Oresteia*, however different in the superficial theatrical effects from those of our day, is the first, and maybe the greatest, of European tragic dramas. To try to render it for the actor's voice, and then to give some permanent record in book form of what we saw as that effect, is possibly the shortest road to grasp it adequately. It is, at any rate, to feel it as a play, and not as a general cultural experience.

David Grene

THE *ORESTEIA:*
INTRODUCTION

David Grene

Perhaps the best way to start is to make a rather simpleminded examination of what is described as the causes of action by different characters, including the Chorus, in the course of the three plays which constitute the *Oresteia*. These three plays are three acts of a single play. This one can be sure of because the last lines of each of the plays clearly refer to the next as a further step. The end of the *Agamemnon* has Clytemnestra saying to Aegisthus, "I / and you together will make all things well, / for we are masters of this house."[1] This certainly looks forward to the return of Orestes, of which we already know from Cassandra's prophecy. In fact, we know that they will surely *not* make all things well, nor will they continue as masters of the house. The second play ends with the choric utterance, "In the beginning was the child-eating / and the sufferings of Thyestes. / Then came the murder of the king, / . . . cut down in his bath. / And now . . . / Is it a rescuer, or must I call him a destruction? / When will it find completion? When will it end? / When will the fierceness of our ruin / fall again to its sleep?"[2] And the last words of the third play are, "For Zeus . . . who Sees All and the Fates / on these terms have come together."[3] These are certainly the three great steps in the fulfillment of fate that Aeschylus bids us observe, and they are contained in the three plays in sequence.

But we find out other things about the causes of the action if we look at what we learn from Clytemnestra in the *Agamemnon*. In conversation with the Chorus after the murder, she claims that she killed Agamemnon because of his sacrifice of their

1. *Agamemnon* 1672–73.
2. *Libation Bearers* 1075.
3. *Eumenides* 1045–46.

I

daughter Iphigeneia. She also speaks of her support from Aegisthus, her lover. Only finally, when the Chorus mentions the "Spirit that attacks the house of the sons of Atreus,"[4] does Clytemnestra declare that indeed she is that spirit, thrice-glutted demon of the house.[5] She is prepared to see herself in this role, bearing her part in the vendetta of family murders. But although in this last function she is the agent of fate, the sacrifice of Iphigeneia and the love of Aegisthus belong also in her motivations. We must add her resentment at Agamemnon's love affair with Cassandra. As an additional factor in the plot, it turns out that Aegisthus is Thyestes' son, and his part in the murder of Agamemnon is largely due to his personal desire for revenge.

The several blocks of events which are the dynamic of fate are, then, if we look at the end of the three plays and Clytemnestra's own assumption of the part of Evil Spirit, the eating of the children, the murder of Agamemnon, the matricide. Yet even at this level of determinism comes Zeus's decision to change something. In this sequence of murder, the killing of Clytemnestra is to have no bloody sequel. The vendetta is to be stopped there by a change in the order of the world. Hitherto, there has been no way in which the blood of the murdered victim would not automatically invoke the Furies who waited on the murdered—provided that the murdered were of blood-kin with the murderer. "The black blood of a man, when once it has fallen to the earth in his death, / who shall conjure it back again?"[6] is a sentiment voiced throughout the plays. But Zeus has decided that there *shall* be such a ritual devised by Apollo, one of the new gods, which will sacramentally abolish the taint of blood. Furthermore, Athena, acting presumably under Zeus's orders, or at least by his sanction, sets up a new legal court of human jurors to investigate the motives of the crimes and the degree of

---

4. *Agamemnon* 1467.
5. Ibid. 1476.
6. *Agamemnon* 1020.

guilt involved. The end of this is to supersede the function of the Furies, who are the representatives of the old gods.

All of this rather confusing scenario is important in the tale Aeschylus is giving us, and also exceedingly important in the world that Aeschylus is going to dissect and dissolve. All great events are partly conditioned by massive movements in a distant past—Fate. But partly also by all sorts of particular motivations working on individuals inside a given situation (Clytemnestra's relations to Iphigeneia, Aegisthus, Cassandra). There is also a set of nonhuman controlling powers *other* than Fate and identifiable as various gods—for example, Zeus or Apollo or Pan.[7] These to a degree can distort the events, even within the pattern of Fate, in time or in their particular shape at least.

Look at the following rather confusing sequence. Agamemnon and Menelaus are likened to vultures robbed of their nestlings.[8] Their complaints are heard by "some" Apollo or Pan or Zeus who treats them as "settlers in his kingdom." So a Lord greater still, Zeus, god of guest-friends, sends the Atreidae against Paris. Here, apparently, the Chorus's sense of the Atreidae as robbed vultures has some particularly illuminating emphasis. In the first place, the assistance is rendered by "some" god, among the three, to the vultures. In the second place, "a Lord greater than the kings, Zeus, god of guest-friends," sends the Atreidae against Troy.

Confusing as this is, in the dual personality of the vultures as birds and as the Atreidae, and in the dual personality of "some Zeus," and so forth, alongside another and greater Zeus, a similar passage a little further on is even more puzzlingly insistent on the doubleness of the agents involved. Two eagles are described in detail,[9] as to their appearance, as the decisive *omen* which sends the Atreidae to Troy. These eagles are seen by Calchas catching

7. *Agamemnon* 55–56.
8. Ibid. 48.
9. Ibid. 114.

and eating a pregnant hare with her unborn brood. Calchas "knew" that the Atreidae *were* the eagles. He then prophesies that Artemis, hating her father's winged hounds for their killing of the hare, will inflict on Agamemnon the disastrous choice of killing his daughter or failing his allies. Because Artemis sees the birds differently, primarily as hare-devourers, they *are* different, they *are* hare-devourers, and she forces the fleet to a standstill by contrary winds and sets the trap for Agamemnon in which he falls and sacrifices his daughter ("to charm the contrariness of Thracian winds"), thereby adding one more reason for Clytemnestra to murder her husband.[10]

So—no sinner is ever free to sin quite freely. He bears with him the weight of the past to which he in a sense belongs. As Virgil says, "*Quisque suos patimur Manes*"—we each one suffer our own ghosts. It is the nexus of motives and past history which carries along with it Clytemnestra, Agamemnon, Aegisthus, Iphigeneia, Orestes, Cassandra. We must add to this weight of the past (which is the main predisposing element of fate) the almost chance and whimsical intervention of those the Greeks called gods. We must also add to the package the voluntary or semivoluntary acts of the individual. When these all converge, you get, in Aeschylus's terms in the *Prometheus Vinctus, kairos,* the moment when all the potentialities converge in action.

Nor is any single great crime free of the weight of the social setting in which it arises. Agamemnon and Menelaus involve their country in total war. The Chorus is composed of old men—there are none left in Argos save the very old and the very young. And Helen and Clytemnestra are sisters and are twin disasters to the two cities to which they came. We must remember Aeschylus's tremendous denunciation of war leaders and all the private lives they wreck. In the last play, the community is again called into the equation—to decide for themselves some of the issues of the past that formerly depended on the private interests of sovereigns. (We remember, too, that alone of the three dra-

10. Ibid. 123–37 and 1420.

matists—Aeschylus, Sophocles, and Euripides—Aeschylus served
several campaigns as a regular soldier.)

What else does this simple separation of the various strands
of causation tell us about the first and second plays in the light
of the third? Surely, the curious but undeniable process of a
growing abstractness, as the play moves from the first to the
second to the third. *Agamemnon* gives you all the complexity of
human action, in its compulsive personal motivation *and* the
force of the past *and* the distorting accidental direction of the
gods' especial will. The second play is very bare. It deals with
the murder of Clytemnestra and Aegisthus to answer the murder
of the king in the *Agamemnon,* but it adds no further motives,
no further characteristics, except the influence on her brother of
the mourning Electra, turned savage murderess. In the *Eumenides,* Orestes alone of those prominent in the first play is alive.
But he is now only a legal defendant in a trial. The issues that
tore our minds apart in the *Agamemnon,* with Clytemnestra
claiming some degree of our sympathy and Agamemnon some
of our pity, have become legal matters and state matters; they
are also turning into basic matters of human behavior in general
terms. The one passionate element is the macabre presentation
of the Furies and the goading influence on them of the nightmare
Clytemnestra. They engage in a symbolic chase after the wretched
Orestes, but, after that, they become prosecutors in the court.
When they become those prosecutors, the issue is the change in
the purification procedure, which implies the new construction
of guilt, and, more doubtfully, the shift from the predominance
of the female to the male in the gods and Attic society.

The *Oresteia* is perhaps the most unusual tragedy in the theater
of the West, and certainly one of the very greatest. But are we
right to call it a tragedy? The *Eumenides* changes the vividness of
the personalization of the characters in the first part of the story.
We were involved with *these* characters, all right, as we might be
in the story of Othello or Macbeth or Julius Caesar. The institutionalization of the court of the Areopagus and the alteration in
the cult and importance of the Furies, and their renaming as the

Kindly Ones, are indeed the follow-up of that first act, the *Agamemnon*. But can we speak of that third act (or third play, if one is literal about it) as a tragic climax? As we speak of the end of *Othello* or *Julius Caesar* or *Macbeth*? Surely, the end of the *Oresteia* might be described as reassuring. The play stops on the note, "For Zeus who Sees All and the Fates / on these terms have come together." Can a tragedy end with a reassurance?

Yet the reassurance lives in the context of issues so huge and a presentation so huge that we catch our breath—as we do at the end of *Lear*, because we and our world are completely involved and because till the last moment the end is in dubious balance. We are present at the untying of elemental knots—how the curse of an unending and inevitable sequence of deaths and blood-guiltiness can be cured; how the shift from the old to the new divinities may imply a whole reevaluation of the male and female in society. How all this is attached to the great figure of Clytemnestra in the first play, so that she is both the agent of the evolution of the story and an example for the third play of what the female of that Amazonian mold could be. In all of this, the solemnity of tragedy is conjured up, and the sense of escape from what so nearly might have been. It is an even vote. What decides it are two factors both connected with sexuality—the pseudoscientific explanation that the mother is only the nurse of the seed, not its parent, and the ambiguous sexual character of the Athena figure, with its emphasis on male, not female. What one has here is the histrionic recreation of a fundamental moment of crisis in man's emotional history at such a depth that our awareness of the issues and the narrow chance separating one conclusion from another constitutes tragic *feeling,* even if we have to differentiate between tragic feeling and tragedy itself.

Part of the difficulty we experience in dealing with the *Oresteia* centers in the *Eumenides*—and this whether we are readers thinking theatrically or an actual audience at a theatrical presentation. The difficulty is there because the actors are nearly exclusively gods. Only Orestes is human, and his dimensions are shrunk to his legal persona. The Furies are demonic, however one decides to put them on the stage. It is indeed the *staging* of the gods, even if the staging is only in our minds, that causes our trouble. In the English-speaking theater we have hardly any tradition of presenting divine figures on the stage. (The medieval miracle and moralizing plays are a long way back and not in our direct theatrical line.) And surprisingly enough, we are without much material on how the Greeks might have thought of doing so at the time of the *Oresteia*. Indeed, through the whole of Greek tragedy, later plays included, there are not many divine figures on the stage. Most of what we have are in Euripides' prologues and epilogues and are not especially objects of mystery or awe. So it is hard for a modern director of a play to say to himself: The Greeks thought of their gods in such a way that their *physical* presentation was naturally *this,* and so we may make of them something like *this.* Yet Apollo, Athena, and the Furies must here appear on the stage as the totally *convincing* histrionic presences which will, between them, bring about the change in purification given as the high orders of Zeus himself and so lead to Athena's institution of the human jury. They must in fact mediate convincingly between the vision of the audience and Aeschylus's ideas. The divine agency involved implies a major break between the old gods and the new. A tremendous weight therefore lies on the coincidence of the deepest feelings of the Athenian audience in regard to gods, and how these gods occur on the stage. One would think the effect of those gods, as the actors played them, must have reserves of dignity and a superior potency emotionally over that of the human figures. Of course, the appeal of the ghost of Clytemnestra to the Furies must have been strong on the side of mystery. It is noteworthy that the masks of these are alleged to have been Aeschylus's special addition and to have been peculiarly terrifying.

The Greeks are without gospel or sacred book. There is moreover hardly an accepted manner of representation of the gods that carries anything like the weight of the Byzantine iconic versions of scenes in the New Testament, whether one takes these on the level of the iconoclasts or their opponents. Herodotus says, "I believe that Hesiod and Homer were four hundred years before my time—and no more than that. It is they who created for the Greeks the theogony [birth of the gods]; it is they who gave to the gods their special names for their descent from their ancestors and divided among them their honors, their arts and their shapes."[11] It is possible, of course, that the legends of a more distant past than that of Homer and Hesiod were carried over in the rites and worship of the gods and may have contributed to the manner of their presentation on the stage. But one wonders, in the face of the statement in Herodotus, which would seem to discountenance just such an idea. The treatment of the gods by Homer and Hesiod is poetic, just as is their treatment of the heroes, as far as claims on our acceptance go. The *Theogonia* of Hesiod embodies many stories older than Hesiod's own period; still, it is pulled together and given coherence by the poet. There is no sacred text. Therefore, artistic treatment claims a total elasticity of response. Aeschylus in the final act of the *Oresteia* is dealing with an element supremely religious; the decision rests with nonhuman powers, but the dramatist is dependent very largely on his own poetic innovation for rendering the moment of the trial, as well as the fact of the trial. True, Athena has the attribute of a kind of androgyny; true, Apollo is the god of healing and prophecy. We know from other sources that Aeschylus's creation of the masks for the Furies was supremely original and terrifying. I think we can be sure that his stage version of Apollo and Athena was equally terrifying, and equally his own.

It is interesting to reflect that in the recent performance of the *Oresteia* at the Court Theatre, Nick Rudall wrestled with the problem of how to produce the necessary awesome effect of the Furies and tried to solve it with an amorphous raiment of sacks, each one covering two Furies, and tried to enhance the further uncanny effect of their movement with trick lights and so forth. He also sought

11. Herodotus, *History* 2.53.

exotic effects in the appearance of Athena in the final scene. He may only have been following what must have been the procedure of Aeschylus himself to achieve a new and completely imaginative effect for the supreme moment of the play. This want of a traditional visual presentation of the gods, at least in more than the simplest of attributes like Athena's aegis or Apollo's prophetic decorations, leads one most probably to the imaginative originality of his treatment of the stories.

If we look at the pattern of transmission of the stages of destiny as they are outlined at the end of *The Libation Bearers,* we must notice how selectively the myth is handled, insofar as the play itself goes. We can also notice how the selection of episodes to bear the chief emphasis is connected, in shadowy fashion, with the parts Aeschylus has failed to emphasize. In the story, of which we have versions elsewhere, and of which Aeschylus himself shows traces, Thyestes seduced Atreus's wife and afterward fled into exile. After some time, Atreus pretended to be reconciled with his brother and invited him home to a feast. At this feast, he furnished Thyestes with the flesh of his sons, whom he, Atreus, had killed. In the play, Aegisthus, who is the son of Thyestes, makes no mention at all of his father's adultery with Atreus's wife. He tells the tale as though Atreus gave the feast of the children unprovoked by any antecedent crime. Only in Cassandra's prophecy, in her frenzied words, is there a reference to the Furies who have "spat in disgust on the brother's bed, that hates its violator."[12] Aeschylus has chosen to break in on the chain of violent crime at a moment which is not exactly the beginning of the sequence. This is to be the abrupt and violent crime which is the hinge on which turns the rest of the dramatic action—which duplicates it. It consists therefore exclusively of murder—after the child-eating. Yet the sexual component of the cannibalistic feast does not quite leave us. Because the murder of the children and the disgustingness of their end, which the

12. *Agamemnon* 1192.

lines stress (notice Thyestes' vomiting),[13] are to be caught up again in the unnatural sacrifice of Iphigeneia by her father, the unnaturalness of the murder of the husband by the wife, of the mother by the son. This line of crime is marked by the purposeful distortion of familial relations. The love of the children by their father, the assumed love of the husband by the wife, becomes the most vulnerable spot in the victim. It is where the cruelty can strike deepest, for it is here that the guards are down. Clytemnestra finds in the murder of Agamemnon and the murder of his mistress Cassandra her strongest sexual satisfaction. The sheer fact of murder answering murder is one thing; the Furies are the servants of this revenge, and as soon as one family murder takes place, another must be there to answer it. But the murder of Cassandra as a "side dish" to Clytemnestra's revenge and the appalling parody of the sex act in Clytemnestra's speech describing her murder of Agamemnon are something else, something additional to the theoretical question of the blood tie in blood-guiltiness. They contribute the personal, voluntary element in Clytemnestra's murder of Agamemnon.

The definition of family relationship as bounded exclusively by the blood tie deliberately ignores the personal sexual relationship between the husband and wife. It is here that Clytemnestra is free and individual in her revenge as none of the other murderers exactly are. Agamemnon is almost forced by the goddess to kill his daughter. Orestes is threatened by Apollo with punishment by his father's Furies if he does not risk the danger from those of his mother. The final horror of Thyestes' feast in the original act of the series is committed by Thyestes in ignorance. But Clytemnestra brings to the murder of her husband an intimate sexual joy in doing the killing and an intimate sexual joy in killing the mistress who loved him and whom he loved, while she herself and *her* lover escaped scot-free. Notice the lines in *The Libation Bearers:* "Who can tell how far those passionate loves / can dare, that live in the minds of perverse women? /

13. Ibid. 1599.

. . . The love-passion of the woman, winning victory, / unloving, perverts the coupling companionship / of beasts and men
alike."[14] Against this are undoubtedly to be set the words of
Apollo when he rejects the claims of the Furies: "In your argument, Aphrodite is discounted utterly— / yet from her the
very dearest things come to human kind; / for man and woman,
the bed, / when justly kept, their fated bed, / is greater than any
oath that can be sworn."[15]

Clytemnestra is truly wounded by the death of her daughter
Iphigeneia, sacrificed by Agamemnon "to charm the contrariness
of Thracian winds."[16] The sacrifice is presented to us as a very
unpleasant option, yet one which Agamemnon finally adopts
rather than fail his allies. Clytemnestra seeks and finds a joy as
personal and uncontrolled in her revenge as his act of violation
of natural feeling was cold-blooded and politic. Sexually, Agamemnon and his mistress will serve her as victims superior to
any more obvious source of gratification. She tries to damn him
spiritually as well as destroy him bodily when she induces him
to walk on the purple carpet—tries and succeeds. The whole
thing is an elaborate play on the dark side of sexuality that the
new order in Athens aims to domesticate or eliminate.

This is how, I think, the passage I have quoted on matrimonial
joy fits in. This matrimony is to be strictly controlled in point
of fidelity and sanctification. Belonging to the same argument,
perhaps, is the effort to reduce absolutely the significance of the
woman in human society. She is the nurse, not the partner in
fertility. There is, symbolically anyway, Athena, unmothered,
all father. Against these must be set, in our theatrical experience
of the play's length, the terrifying element of Clytemnestra's
sexual drive, twisted, perverse, but deeply recognizable—because we understand her as a complex human being in the first
play more than anyone else throughout the trilogy. Maybe also

14. *Libation Bearers* 600 ff.
15. *Eumenides* 218 ff.
16. *Agamemnon* 1420.

in a somewhat similar way we should remember the wolfish Electra, driven by her intense love of her dead father to the enjoyment of the murder of her mother and Aegisthus.

Is there in this a dimension to the Furies that is not confined to the championship of the blood-tie in vengeance, a dimension opposed to the new order of rational determination of such matters as the family? The Furies represent, poetically, dark qualities associated with the underworld; they have no proper links with the gods and are dreaded and rejected by men. They are "a dreadful troop of women. / No, I won't say they were women, but Gorgons. / No, not that, either; their shapes did not seem to me / like Gorgons' shapes. . . . These I saw now / were wingless, black and utterly repulsive. / They snored, the smell of their breaths was not to be borne, / and from their eyes there trickled a loathsome gum."[17]

These figures stand for something frightening in *femaleness,* though they are not exactly women. They are the exaggerated, imaginative, nightmare expression of what is terrifying in Clytemnestra herself as she stands over her dead husband and remembers the three blows with which she killed him and was invaded by the stream of his blood, in which she "rejoiced as much as the new-sown earth / rejoices in the glad rain of Zeus, / when the buds strike in earth's womb."[18] The act of Clytemnestra, however horrible, is one we can recognize as part of what our human experience warrants, the substitution of sadistic cruelty for sex. The image of the Furies extends that understanding beyond the dramatic experience of Clytemnestra to a terrifying phantom life of twisted emotion. And the blood tie the Furies follow so obediently gains an added chapter when they speak to the cowering Orestes as "a shade, / the blood sucked from you, fodder for ghosts."[19] It it too fanciful to see the final conflict of

17. *Eumenides* 47 ff.
18. *Agamemnon* 1392.
19. *Eumenides* 302.

the play between this mythic phantom life of the Furies against the idealized phantom image of the unmothered Athena?

It is a pity from our point of view as dramatic readers or viewers that the kind of social rationality which opposes the Furies is bolstered by the pseudoscientific theory about the mother as the mere nurse of the seed, or by the mystical sexual character of the divine figure of Athena. These are for Aeschylus common dramatic presentations of convincing arguments against the order of the Furies, with its construction of kindred blood as base.

Such arguments as part of the winning case at the trial may indeed oppose the Furies themselves in their embodiment of their theatrical position in the society. But they hardly touch the terrors associated with the Furies, which we are shown when Apollo talks of them as the proper companions of the scenes of torture—the eye gouging, the castrations, the fingernail extractions, and so on. They are women and not women, Gorgons and not Gorgons. They haunt the mind with some suggestion of femaleness, and some suggestions of the monstrous. Somehow, the old sanctions belong to a world of emotions gone wrong. Their champions rejoice in bloodletting, in vampirism, as the proper response to the recovery of bloodshed. But they recognize only blood in the common body of mother and son and father and child. They see no crime, nor compulsion to avenge, in the murderous violation of sexual love or affection in themselves. The more human and voluntary the emotions, the less they concern the Furies.

But the end of this trial looks both ways, toward the defeat, but not the complete defeat, of the Furies, and this Athena herself stresses. The votes are equal. The *human* judges think, as many on the one side as the other, that Orestes was right or wrong. By implication, the Furies' contention, "There is a place where terror is good," is equally accepted and rejected.

Can the dark terrors which rode on the underside of man's mind, when the Furies enjoyed their ritual intervention in his affairs, be checked, while some more wholesome blend of the rational and the mystical be maintained?[20] Can this vendetta of hatred and vengeance, reveling in increasing the horrors and tortures, be managed in some sort of harmony with a human community? Athena says it can—by a sort of domestication of the Furies. They will no longer be an autonomous force summoned by the act of murder, itself circumscribed by the ties of blood kinship. Instead, the human jury will decide on the balance of act and motive, and according to a new social hierarchy. That is, the new court of the Areopagus will do all this, *if* it follows the precedent of how it deals with Orestes, when Athena establishes it.

What remains doubtful is how the human jury, which clearly displaces the Furies in the murder trial, is going to interact with them. Athena spends all her persuasive force in the rest of the play inducing the Furies to bless Athens instead of cursing it. The more general question raised by the Furies' argument, "There is a place where terror is good," drifts out of sight except for a somewhat vague reference: "They bring to perfection for all to see / what they have provided; / for some, occasions for song; / for others, a life rich in tears."[21] In some general way, not really clear to us, the Furies, according to Athena's offer, are to be given a supervisory power over the morals and manners of society, especially in matters of human fertility.[22] This is the compensation the Furies receive for their defeat in the trial of Orestes, and all that this implies for them.

Finally it is very important that the Furies *are* induced not to punish Athens for their defeat, and that they are offered and accept the makeweight award. It is important for the way the Greeks saw justice and history. The defeated must not be driven to desperation, especially when as in this instance the defeated are connected with such powerful underlying emotions. Hence,

20. *Agamemnon* 696–99.
21. *Eumenides* 952.
22. Ibid. 835, 895.

the Furies are escorted to their new "home" beneath the earth in Athenian territory, of which they are now benevolent patrons.

There is one other issue, more shadowy than the foregoing but still haunting the play. The Furies claimed that they were the champions of the old ways which "you young gods have ridden down. / You have snatched them out of my hands."[23] The Furies are feminine, daughters of Night.[24] Apollo and Zeus are masculine, and Athena ostentatiously supports Apollo in his claim for her unmothered status by asserting that she is wholly her father's, with no sympathy with her femaleness, of whatever kind it may be. One should notice that at the beginning of the *Eumenides,* when the priestess of Apollo cites the history of the oracle of Delphi, it is in the possession of Earth, Themis, and Phoebe, in succession. After that it goes to Phoebus, the first male. The priestess also goes out of her way to add that the succession was voluntary, no force involved. Phoebe is of course the feminine form of the masculine Phoebus, and the change in the name is also stressed. The conclusion of the *Eumenides* shows a further transfer of power from female divinities to male. Again the change is made, at the last anyway, voluntarily. Was there really at some prehistoric period a shift from female to male gods, and could Aeschylus have conceivably had knowledge of it? Or is it all an invention of his extraordinary imagination? We simply do not know, but the comparison of the two passages, that dealing with Delphi and that with the Furies, rather suggests that he wanted us to notice the similarity of the process. Finally, if there were such a shift from female to male gods, either in prehistory or in Aeschylus's dramatic fantasy, did he feel that, connected with such a change in the divinities, there was a *moment* when Attic human society shifted its emphasis of importance from female to male, and that the true image of *that* was his own description of the trial of Orestes?

23. Ibid. 808.
24. Ibid. 820.

THE *ORESTEIA*:
THE THEATRICAL PERSPECTIVE

Nicholas Rudall

It would be well, I think, to speak first of origins. In 1984 the Court Theatre, where I am the artistic director, had previously commissioned David Grene and Wendy O'Flaherty to do a translation of Sophocles' *Antigone*. In the course of our conversations before and during that translation and that production, certain questions were raised about the specific problems of translating an ancient tongue for a modern performance. These questions, which I shall shortly discuss, were in a sense quite new to all three of us. For although we could all read Greek and had all done translations, writing for a specific project was new. In retrospect, the association was successful. The translation revealed the tragic and indeed the comic colors of Sophocles' elusive style. But in a real sense it was a practice clinic for the Everest of Greek dramatic literature.

When the theater decided to do the *Oresteia,* it was natural to renew the collaboration. The questions were raised again. What should be the dominant *tone* of the translation? Victoriana being rejected a priori, we felt that contemporaneity, however limpid and elegant, was equally unattractive. I stress the word "contemporaneity"—not "colloquialism," which would have been unthinkable, but accessible modern poetic prose that read with a modern eloquence. This was tacitly rejected for reasons dictated by Aeschylus's style and by the demands of a modern production. Aeschylus's style, as Aristophanes testifies,[1] was alien and often inaccessible to his contemporaries. He loved to carve words of granite or of air, and so it was felt that the translation should reflect this.

1. In the *Frogs*.

As for the theatrical demands, some were echoes of the Sophocles collaboration, while others were quite new. The most difficult demand is the one I believe is answered most brilliantly in this translation. As the stage director, I referred to it (to myself alone) as distanced accessibility. Let me explain this idea since it was an idea which was to inform the whole production. The *Oresteia,* as indeed all Greek drama, contains lengthy passages of quite treacherous modernity; for example, the herald's unromantic and dispassionate account of life under the walls, or the words of Orestes' nurse, both in her famous memory speech (Did Shakespeare know it when he wrote *Romeo and Juliet?*) and in her brief but telling dialogue with the Chorus. Such passages invite the trappings of a "psychological" production, one in which motive and subtext flicker constantly beneath the skin of the words. What we needed was a language which told the audience: These are human beings who lived and felt and sometimes thought as we live and feel and think.

But they did so in a time out of mind. They are myth. Furthermore, one of the major musical movements of Aeschylus's symphony is the development of cognition. The characters, whether divine, choric, or human, are constantly confronting the unknown and the unnamed. For example, one actual process of the drama is the discovery of the meaning of matricide. So the language had to seem, frequently, predominantly, new-coined yet ancient. A living myth, distanced accessibility. Otherwise, the treachery of a misperceived modernity would have made itself quickly apparent in production.

How to handle a chorus? David was concerned that they not walk around in "those bloody bedsheets and masks." I was concerned that the three choruses had so much to say that was not technically "conversation." The modern audience is not used to lectures, however poetic. In the event, practical solutions emerged to solve both our misgivings during production. But at this stage of preparation we all agreed that the solution was a peculiar faithfulness to the text. In other words, "poetry" was not to be made in English through meter or elevation of style but through a rigorous and truthful literalness. For example, "The overold, the leafage already withering, / walks his three-footed way, no stronger than a child; / wanders, a dream in the daylight."[2] That is very like the Greek. Yet it is prose. It is very nearly poetry. It is distant, yet it is accessible. Speak it aloud but once.

Finally, it was agreed that Wendy and David would translate the complete text. I promised to cut what I could not stage, not knowing what those cuts would be nor whether they would be surgical or savage.

The translation evolved over the year. My brief collaborations served only as unnecessary stimuli for what seemed to be a remarkably fluid process. When the complete text was in my hands, I was sure that here were words meant to be spoken on stage.

So I began the second stage—the first attempts to conceive of a production that would live comfortably in a small (255-seat) modern theater. Although we had determined that all three plays would be performed in one evening, I had as yet no idea how to compress the action, nor was it at all clear what should be cut. I began to meet with my set— and costume—designer, Linda Buchanan, my lighting designer, Rita Pietrozyk, and my associate director, Nick Faust. This was almost six months before we were to begin rehearsal. These meetings forged the final shape of the production. I was the only one who knew the plays at all well. This turned out to be a remarkably helpful stroke of luck. I was compelled time and time again to explain not only the symbolism but the very plot. And my explanations were seized upon and made concrete.

Let me give some examples. If one reduces the watchman's function at the beginning of the *Oresteia* to its essence, it is this: he is waiting and watching for a light which will illuminate what should perhaps be left in darkness. This meant a still figure perched above the house, eyes and face illuminated by the flicker of a small fire, the rest darkness. That is what the audience saw

2. *Agamemnon* 80–82.

as it came in. Then the flame would flicker, and a different source, far away, would light up the stage, the watchman would beat an enormous gong, and then, as suddenly as his fear descended, so would the darkness. In fact, the shadow of an eagle darkened the stage.

The stage. Our conceptual meetings finally gave us the following stage design. The forestage was to be of sand. Immediately behind it would be the apparently solid fore-wall of a structure. When lit, it became translucent. Behind this was the physical set proper, a series of angled platforms connected by flights of stairs. The platforms went from four feet above stage level to eight feet to twelve feet to twenty feet. It was to be a pale grayish white, so that it would reflect light and color. It was to be neutral enough to change character for each play when the lights gave it a new mood or even shape. It was indeed to be a character.

To resume. When the watchman leaves, he suggests that all would not be well if only the house could speak. The opaque walls would become translucent. Within the house a trio of old men, all white, would begin the tale of Aeschylus's first chorus. I will not describe many other scenes in detail, but I will take one major example from each play to illustrate how design and performance evolved. The greatest difficulty for a contemporary audience, unversed in Greek myth, is to grasp the connection between the death of Iphigeneia and the death of Agamemnon. It is difficult because it is unspoken in the play. Furthermore, a modern audience is not going to grasp the full significance of the purple cloth upon which Agamemnon walks to his death. At the end of the first chorus, there is an account of the sacrifice of Iphigeneia. It is an elusive, impressionistic account which ends at the moment before slaughter: "What happened after that I neither saw nor tell." In a series of conversations with the designers and Nick Faust, I explained that the murder of the daughter, however necessary, was linked to the act of walking on purple. To walk on purple meant, on one level, to behave with excessive arrogance, but on another, it symbolized another, greater "arrogance": the shedding of the purple blood of his daughter. We made the following stage picture. As the Chorus spoke of Iphigeneia, the audience saw on the topmost platform a series of brief tableaux: Iphigeneia in her wedding robe, Agamemnon's arrival at the altar, the sword at the throat, and then, when the Chorus said, "What happened after that I neither saw nor tell," Agamemnon cut his daughter's throat. From that part of the "altar" there issued a stream of purple silk which flowed down thirty feet of steps, finally coming to rest on the ground level below. It was about five feet wide, and it simply flowed from the top to the bottom. (It was technically quite difficult and, indeed, treacherously and dramatically failed to come off in several preview trials.) When Agamemnon was later tempted by Clytemnestra to tread upon "purple," her handmaidens merely extended this cloth to his carriage, and when he stepped down he stepped into his daughter's blood, and when he walked the flights of steps to his death, he walked in his daughter's blood (to the place of his daughter's slaughter).

In *The Libation Bearers,* it is difficult to comprehend the relationships among the Chorus, Electra, and Orestes in that first long scene. What I said to our group was that, whereas in *Agamemnon* we had a chorus of free men who took no action, here we had a chorus of slave women who were prepared to act. Once Electra and Orestes recognize each other, there evolves a complex and poetic scene in which Orestes finds the strength to kill his mother. The problem was how to make this clear. It was staged at the sandy grave of the father. Electra is manic, pathologically suspicious, obsessively bent on revenge. That is how she was played in this production. Orestes, although determined, is occasionally lost and afraid. The Chorus is active in its urgency. It was clear to me that the prayers at the grave were meant to transfer the power of the father to the son. It was necessary to make this concrete for the audience. At the grave, the women drive the children to a frenzy, until finally the grave bleeds. Orestes touches the blood and places it upon his forehead and lips and upon Electra's lips. From here on, Electra speaks no more, and Orestes takes charge, gives orders, and formulates his plan. By finding a theatrically concrete symbol, we were again able to convey the meaning of at least part of that extraordinary scene.

It would be possible to take many examples of this conceptual process from the *Eumenides,* for it posed many problems. I shall take but one. How could we physically represent the Furies? Aeschylus gives us the brilliant stroke of having the priestess reenter on her knees after seeing them. (We had no priestess in the final version.) She then describes them in vivid and gory detail. The description is so precise that it needs no imaginative additions. The images of hounds, snakes, vultures, claws, blood, and pus are astonishingly repellent. But they are also an impossible amalgam to make concrete on the stage. Presumably, Aeschylus, having so described them, presented them visually in a far less spectacular way. The Greek tragic convention, which clearly described deaths but rarely showed them, applied here too.

There was no satisfactory single answer for the modern stage. We chose to address the following problems: How do we make the distinction between the gods of the underworld and Apollo and Athena? What is one essential quality of the Furies? To answer the first question, we decided that the gods of the underworld would always be in half-darkness and would physically shrink from any source of light. Apollo's sunlight was a potentially dangerous weapon. To answer the second question was more difficult. I finally decided that the essential quality of the Furies was a frightening ability to change shape. Perhaps one quality of their terror was to be found in the unknown. In the event, four—it was to have been six—actors were placed in two separate bags made of a gray stretch fabric that was streaked with red. After not enough rehearsal, they were able to take on extraordinary shapes. It would be wasted labor to attempt to describe their contortions. Their voices came from changing locales—fragmented, orchestrated sentences, deep voices, shrill voices, calm voices. This was predominantly Nick Faust's work, and thus I can claim a proportional objectivity and argue that it was an astonishingly inventive attempt to solve a problem that with twice the number of actors and twice the theatrical resources would have remained incredibly difficult.

The rehearsal. A glimpse. We sat, thirteen actors and the rest of us, around a table, for four days, eight hours a day. I began to cut, to explain. The language seemed, surprisingly, quite easy for them to grasp. We talked about Greece and kinship and matricide and Furies, of gods and graves and scholars. As all good actors are, they were afraid of it. It seemed so huge, so impenetrable. The language was distancing them. They were afraid of that. They were contemporary American actors gifted at realism, authenticity of emotion and thought. They were used to dialogue where ideas and motives shift and are shifted constantly. Here there is no dialogue except brief, unnatural, stichomythia. (Sticho what?). Alternating single lines of dialogue. Ah. How did Clytemnestra feel about the return? Why would Agamemnon bring his mistress back with him, right there in the carriage? Mainly, How can we possibly make these creatures human?

We began rehearsals in late summer, and after we had sat for four days and beaten a primitive version into shape, it was time to get to our feet. Nick Faust and I had decided that the actors must have a chance to discover the reality of the events told in an alien tongue and in an alien form. We were both suspicious of free improvisation. It was decided that we *would* improvise, but in the following way: each actor had to say *every* line that the character he or she was playing spoke, but no line could be spoken until it was understood in emotional and human terms. It was a hot day when we began and by chance the rehearsal hall was locked. Adjacent was a quiet, unkempt tract of land with bushes, brown grass, and sand. I decided we would begin with *The Libation Bearers*. I marked out a convenient depression in the dirt as the grave site. Nick Faust and I said we would interrupt if necessary, whisper to actors already in a scene and to those about to enter. We had no idea of what the next two days would bring.

Orestes and Pylades entered—that is, they came from across the park. They were cautious. Pylades took charge—the actor had served in Vietnam. It was eerie and unsettling. But we were not quite prepared for what happened for the next two and a half hours, in which we covered only 550 lines of the play. Some impressions: Orestes stood above the grave for what seemed like an eternity. There was only the hot wind. Pylades was nervous. Finally, Orestes spoke and you knew that here, beneath the earth, were the bones of the father he had never really known. He touched the earth and cleared away debris. And he began to weep quietly. As he wept, the women walked toward the grave; unconsciously, they began to chant and moan. The sound was strange, again eerie. Orestes and Pylades left but listened nearby. Electra stood apart as the women improvised a ritual. The discovery of the hair and the footprint—terror, laughter—meant a long and reasoned examination of Electra's private fears, and when Orestes was finally and fully believed, we all sat on the earth, and we shared the fullness of Aeschylus's genius. For everything human and beautiful was there in that alien tongue and alien form. Seven years of anger and anguish dissolved into the tears of a brother and a sister and some women who loved them. And it *was* real after all, profoundly real.

Once these first hours had passed and we all knew that we were discovering the reality of the play, some magnificent moments emerged from this improvisatory game. Clytemnestra struggling among the old men, or making Electra comb her hair. The herald, of all people, becoming a full character, who kissed his mother earth, poured the dirt over his hair, kissed the first woman (who bought him milk to drink) with awe and tenderness, found his father in the Chorus, and wept as he remembered those who had died. I will also not forget the moment after the death of Agamemnon, when Aegisthus and Clytemnestra embraced as the Chorus left, and out of the blue came Electra, clawing, spitting, weeping—already, without knowing it, a pre-figuration of Euripides' psychopath. Nor will I forget how the choruses came alive when forced to *mean* what they said; how free men skulked and slave women beat the earth in an attempt to raise the dead.

Not all of this mayhem survived to the staging of the play. Much did. But we all knew that we were in the presence of a magnificent writer who could capture the essence of the real in a nonrealistic form. That gave the actors courage but also made them aware of the difficulty. The performance was never the same twice, even long after opening night; problems were solved, new problems created, new ideas tried out, rejected, tried again. It is hard to judge—and perhaps inappropriate for me of all people to judge—what was finally achieved. But at the end of the run, there was not a ticket to be had for love or money.

TRANSLATING FOR THE STAGE AND FROM THE STAGE

Wendy Doniger O'Flaherty

I intend these brief comments as a kind of connecting supplement to the longer essays of David Grene and Nicholas Rudall, linking the insights derived from my simultaneous confrontations with the problems of translation and with the problems of a stage production. Together, these two encounters, and those two men, taught me a great deal about a play that I thought I had known pretty well when we agreed to undertake the new translation.

Producing a translation that I knew would be spoken on a stage forced me not only to conceive of each line as it would sound aloud but also to conceive of it as a line that could be comprehended at first hearing by an audience. This meant that we had to iron out all ambiguities of construction (the kinds of things that commas sort out on the printed page) as well as ambiguities of sound (for example, given the strongly sexual nature of the play, and in particular of our translation of it, we decided *not* to refer to sailors as seamen). It also led to major disagreements between David Grene (an Anglo-Irishman) and me (American born and bred) about what one had a right to expect of an *American* audience. We fought long and hard over "gravid load of leverets," I torn between our love of the line (and the feeling that "pregnant belly full of baby bunnies" somehow did not do the trick) and our fear that "leveret" was not a word bandied about by your man or woman on the street. The actors worried about it too, and we produced a paler but clearer version for them; but we were delighted to hear, sitting in the audience on opening night, that at the eleventh hour the actors had come to grips with the line, and "gravid load of leverets"[1] was heard in some, though not all, performances.

1. *Agamemnon* 118.

But the knowledge that we were translating for a stage production affected the choice of words in other ways, too. In the
course of our many conversations with Nick Rudall and as we
began to understand his vision of the play—and I do mean *vision,*
the way it would *look*—I came to have a new feeling for the
visual component of Aeschylus's imagery. At all the crucial junc-
tures where the Greek could legitimately be translated in so many
different ways, I found myself leaning toward those ways that
conjured up colors, shapes, parts of the body, physical objects.
And as I began more and more to imagine what the line would
look like, as well as sound like, I began to notice patterns in the
Greek that I had never noticed before.

Take the blood, for instance, an element of central importance
to the play. Nick's inspiration to use the purple silk for Iphigeneia's blood made me see links among the sacrificial, royal,
and sexual imagery that I had previously overlooked. Explicitly,
it literally connects the (purple) blood that flows from Iphigeneia
when Agamemnon kills her with the purple carpet that Clytemnestra seduces Agamemnon to walk upon, the blood of sacrifice
with the purple blood royal (what we call the "blue blood" of
nobility), the "blood" of the family lineage with the blood of
the marital murder. By extension, the translation of blood into
a piece of blood-red *cloth* stimulates the imagination to forge
another link with another piece of cloth: the rich robe that traps
Agamemnon in the bath where Clytemnestra stabs him[2]—perhaps purple to begin with, and certainly purple with his blood
at the end.

This purple cloth then reappears when Orestes begins to go
mad after murdering his mother and Aegisthus. When he begins
to talk about traps and fetters and garments, we might at first
think that he is displaying the robe in which he has just murdered
Aegisthus, having trapped the trapper in his own sort of trap,
one of the dominant themes of the play. But then Orestes begins
to justify himself by recollecting his mother's murder of his

2. *Ibid.* 1383.

father, and then Orestes *sees* another bloody robe, the robe in which his father was trapped in the bath. This cloth is purple with Agamemnon's blood and, by the chain of associations, with Iphigeneia's blood. The purple dye has become a very complex embroidery indeed:

> And look you, now, those that have heard the sad story,
> look at the traps for my poor father, the tyings of his feet,
> the fetters of his hands, the linkage of his legs.
> Spread the garment out, and show it to all that stand
> around here: this was the covering of the man.[3]

> This robe is my witness
> that the sword of Aegisthus stained it.
> Time has deepened the stain of murdered blood
> that, joining in, has spoiled
> the many other dyes in the embroidery.[4]

The reference to time, and to the dyes in the embroidery—that precious royal purple of which Clytemnestra boasted to have such an overabundance—clearly suggests that, in the mind of Orestes at least, this is the robe of Agamemnon. And indeed, in some of the performances of the play, the actor playing Orestes held in his hand a piece of cloth distinctively marked like the robe that we last saw upon the shoulders of Agamemnon in *Agamemnon*.

But is it in fact that robe? Is it reasonable to suppose that Orestes somehow actually found, upon his return years later, the robe in which Agamemnon was murdered? Perhaps. Electra might have saved it (it is just the sort of obsessive, vengeful, psychotic thing that she would do). And we know that Orestes saved, for many years, another piece of cloth, one that Electra had woven on her loom;[5] indeed, Orestes used that manufactured cloth as a piece of crucial evidence to prove his own identity, more convincing even than the *natural* evidence provided by his footprints and his hair, even as he is now attempting to use the

3. *Libation Bearers* 980–84.
4. *Ibid.* 1011–14.
5. *Ibid.* 231.

"robe in which Agamemnon was murdered" as crucial evidence. But could this not be the robe of Aegisthus, which Orestes' disturbed mind has conflated with the other robe in which Aegisthus murdered his father? Has the blood of Aegisthus "joined in" and "spoiled" the "other dye"—the stain made by the blood of Agamemnon upon the mind of Orestes? Or, finally, is there any robe there at all? We know that Orestes is going mad and, in particular, that his madness leads him to *see* things that no one else sees; only a few lines later he acknowledges that he can see the Furies, while no one else sees them. Perhaps he sees a robe, too, that no one else can see. Only when I myself *saw* the actor holding the cloth did I realize how very strange and ambiguous this scene was. On the one hand, no one could possibly know precisely how to translate the ambiguous words into unambiguous visual images. And yet, on the other hand, only by seeing those visual images could one fully realize the meaning of some of those words and conjure up, simultaneously and wordlessly, several different, vital episodes of the play.

But on a yet more abstract level, the concretization of the metaphor of blood brings out another important series of correspondences, between the sexual act and the act of murder. Clytemnestra's false boast that she no more knows how to take pleasure in another man than she knows "how to dip this blade to temper it"[6] is later echoed in her confession of the masculine sexual pleasure that she derives from plunging the knife into Agamemnon. For when Clytemnestra says that Agamemnon "poured out a sharp stream of his blood / and struck me with the dark bloody shower. / I rejoiced as much as the new-sown earth / rejoices in the glad rain of Zeus, / when the buds strike in earth's womb,"[7] she is not merely prefiguring the nightmare bloodthirstiness of the Furies, as David Grene has rightly pointed out in his essay. She is reenacting the very birth of the Furies themselves, giving birth to them again on the stage. For, ac-

6. *Agamemnon* 612.
7. *Ibid.* 1390–94.

cording to Hesiod, the Furies were born of a similarly perverse sexual act: when Cronos castrated his father Ouranos, the severed organ itself, as is well known, was thrown into the ocean and gave birth to Aphrodite. But there was another birth from that action, an inverse shadow of the creation of the goddess of erotic love: the drops of blood that gushed forth from the wound were received by the Earth, Gaia (mother of Cronos and wife of the mutilated Ouranos), who gave birth to the Furies and the Giants.[8] In choosing such sexually charged words to celebrate her own murder of Agamemnon, Clytemnestra implicitly likens her act to the castration of Ouranos by Cronos (fated to be in his turn overcome by his son Zeus, whom Clytemnestra invokes in the same line). In calling up the image of the fertilizing drops of blood in the earth, she thus simultaneously visualizes the past murder as a castration and foreshadows the future appearance of the Furies as the children of her own tormented imagination. This connection between the Furies and the sexual mutilation of men is further supported by Apollo's statement that the Furies belong in places where there are "the gouging of eyes, / cutting of throats, castration of young boys, / mutilation, stoning; where the whimperings / of men impaled cry pity." They also threaten to blight human fertility by shedding drops of poison on the earth.[9] The Earth which is both the home and the womb of the Furies is fertilized not by rain nor by seed but by the blood of the destruction of seed.

In addition, the implications of Clytemnestra's speech assimilating blood to seed set the stage for one of the most peculiar, and for me most unpalatable, parts of the play: the argument, in the *Eumenides,* that the mother is related to her husband but not related to her child. Clytemnestra's violent metaphor is, ironically, the embodiment of the shadow side of the very argument that will be her undoing, and the undoing of the Furies, in the third play.

8. Hesiod, *Theogony* 183–85.
9. *Eumenides* 187–90 and 782–84.

In that play, the Furies begin by arguing that the husband is not related to the wife but the son *is* related by blood to his mother:

> Furies: She was no blood kin to him she killed.
> Orestes: *I* am blood kin, then, to my mother?
> Furies: How else did she raise you, murderer, in her womb?[10]

This seemed to me a pretty conclusive argument. But Apollo sees things differently. First, he implies that the bond of the marriage bed, "greater than any oath that can be sworn,"[11] outranks all other bonds. Then he states outright that the bond between mother and child is no bond at all: "She that is called the mother of the child / is not its parent, but the nurse of the new seed; / it is the stallion's thrust that is the parent; / the woman saves the young living plant for a stranger."[12] This argument, which seems to violate not only observed obstetrical facts but human decency, is in fact widely attested in Indo-European mythology: the woman is merely the field in which the man sows his seed, and the child owes all of his (*sic*) qualities to the man alone.[13]

But the ancient metaphor suddenly takes on new meaning in the light of Clytemnestra's earlier words. For, by murdering Agamemnon in a manner which she perversely analogizes to the sexual act, she has simultaneously established a literal *blood tie* between herself and her husband (his blood joining them together sexually in a way that, according to the theory of Apollo, his semen never could) and grotesquely distorted the unfair agricultural analogy that would make her nothing but a field upon which he rains his blood-seed. Seeing that piece of purple silk made me see the link between those passages. Perhaps this is simply saying, at too great a length, that one cannot understand a play without seeing it in a truly inspired production as well as by reading it in a careful translation.

10. *Ibid.* 605–10.
11. *Ibid.* 218ff.
12. *Ibid.* 657–61.
13. See Wendy Doniger O'Flaherty, *Women, Androgynes, and Other Mythical Beasts* (Chicago: University of Chicago Press, 1980).

PART ONE
UNABRIDGED TRANSLATION

AGAMEMNON

DRAMATIS PERSONAE

Sentry

Chorus,
old men of Argos left behind
after the Argives went to Troy

Clytemnestra,
queen of Argos in the absence
of King Agamemnon at Troy

Herald from the Greek army

King Agamemnon

Cassandra,
princess of Troy, daughter
of King Priam

Aegisthus

AGAMEMNON

Sentry

    You gods, release me.
    Crouched like a dog, I watch always, all year long,
    on the tower of the sons of Atreus.
    I have come to know the nightly gathering of the stars
    and those radiant dynasts of the firmament that lead them.
    They bring winter and summer to men.
    Now I watch for a flaming light,
    the beacon fire, the tell-tale witness that Troy is captured.
    Such are my orders, orders from a hopeful queen   10
    who thinks with the mind of a man.
    I have a bed here, soaked with dew, always shifting.
    But no dreams. Fear is my visitor, not sleep.
    I cannot close my eyes for fear.
    Sometimes I whistle or hum;
    the tunes are my drug against my sleepiness.
    But then the sorrow comes.
    This house is in bitter trouble.
    Once it was well governed; not now.
    Still, may the fire of good news light the darkness   20
    to be the lucky release from our troubles.

    The beacon! Day out of night!
    The dances everywhere in Argos!
    Thanks, good beacon!
    My lady, Agamemnon's wife, get out of bed!
    Cry aloud a blessing on this beacon,   30
    since Troy is surely captured.
    I will myself begin the dance, for I'll score to myself, too,
    the winning dice that the beacon threw for my master.
    Oh, that I could touch with this hand of mine
    the hand that I love, my lord's.
    As for the rest, I haven't a word;
    a great ox stands on my tongue.

If the house itself had a voice to speak,
it would tell the clearest story.
I choose to speak to those who understand;
for the others, I am all forgetfulness.

Chorus

This is the tenth year   40
since they launched from this land
the Greek fleet of a thousand ships
to help right wrongs done.
They launched it, King Menelaus,
great plaintiff against Priam,
and Agamemnon his brother;
twin the yoke joining them in honor and throne,
twin their shared grace of God.

From their hearts the great war cry;   50
they screamed like eagles,
that wheel and wheel high above their eyries,
driven by the oarage of their wings,
in lonely agony for the loss of their nestlings,
and all the watchful care they had spent guarding them.

But One yet higher up, some Apollo or Pan or Zeus,   60
hears the shrill-voiced sorrow of these settlers in his kingdom
and sends on the evildoers
the Fury that brings punishment, however late.
So a Lord greater than the kings, Zeus god of guest-friends,
sends the sons of Atreus on Alexander;
in this quarrel over a woman of many men,
he would lay upon Greeks and Trojans alike
many wrestlings where the limbs grow heavy
and the knee is pressed into the dust
and the spear is shattered in the first rites of engagement.
Yet it is now as it is.
Fulfillment moves toward what is fated.

And not with burnt offerings nor with pouring on of wine   70
nor sacrifice to the gods below
will you assuage that stubborn anger.

But we, dishonored for the ancientness of our flesh,
were left behind then when the army went;
we remain, propping on staffs a strength like a child's.
For the child's marrow, too, leaps within his breast
but is only the match of an old man's;
the god of war is not there either.
And the overold, the leafage already withering,   80
walks his three-footed way, no stronger than a child;
wanders, a dream in the daylight.

You, daughter of Tyndarus, Queen Clytemnestra,
What's the matter? What's the news? What have you heard?
What message do you trust, that you order sacrifices
at all the altars?
Of all the gods that hold our city,
of those above and those beneath the earth,
of those at the doorpost and those at the marketplace,
the altars blaze with offerings.
Here one torch sends its flames to the sky,   90
and another raises its light,
charmed by the soft, guileless urgings of pure streams of oil
drawn from the depth of the royal store.
Tell us what you can and what may be said
about all these things.
Cure this care that now broods darkly on our minds.
But then hope, shining out of the sacrifice,   100
turns away the insatiable thoughts that might otherwise
eat out the heart in sorrow.

It is mine to declare the omens of victory
given to princely men on the journey.
For by God's grace, old age, which grows with life, my life,

still breathes on my lips persuasion,
the strength of song.
I tell how the princes of the Achaeans,
twin-throned, single-hearted
lords of the youth of Greece,
were sent against the land of Troy
with spear in hand to exact vengeance.
The furious omen-birds sent them,   110
one black eagle, one white-tail,
the kings of birds to the kings of the ships.
Near the palace they came on the spear-striking side,
perched where all could see them
as they fed on the womb's gravid load of leverets,
mother and all, pulled down in the hare's last course.
Cry sorrow, sorrow, but let the good prevail.   120

Yet the honest prophet of the army saw
the two sons of Atreus,
twin in military spirit,
and knew the princely leaders and hare-devourers—
knew that they were one and the same.
And so he declared in his prophecy,
"In time, this journey will capture Troy, Priam's city;
and all the communal herds that graze before her towers
shall Fate give violently to plunder.
I only pray that no anger from the God will cast a cloud   130
upon this army forged from before to be
a great iron bit in the mouth of Troy.
For Queen Artemis is full of pity out of jealousy
against those winged hounds of her father
who devour in sacrifice
the unhappy cowering mother with her brood
before they come to birth.
She hates the eagles' feast.
Cry sorrow, sorrow, but let the good prevail.

38

Yes, she is kindly, that beautiful one,   140
to cubs, scarcely crawling, of savage lions,
and she finds her delight in all the breast-loving infants
of wild things of the field.
Yet she grants fulfillment of what the omens imply:
grant, Lady, favorable fulfillment, and void the other.
I call on Apollo the Healer
to keep her from setting against the Greeks
those contrary winds, winds that hold ships,
staying winds, winds that stop sailing altogether.
She might do this in eagerness for a different sacrifice,
one that is lawless and horrible,
a trueborn craftsman of quarrels,
that has no awe of a husband.
For full of terrors it lurks,   150
house keeping, crafty, long-memoried,
an anger that punishes child-slaughter."

Such were the prophecies of Calchas's voice,
mingled with the good things,
and all predicted for our royal house
from omens on the way.
In harmony with these,
cry sorrow, sorrow, but let the good prevail.

Zeus, whoever he is,   160
if it is dear to him to be so called,
this is how I call him.
I have thrown all into the scale,
but cannot find his likeness—
there is only Zeus,
if I must cast my burden of vain care from the heart
in honest truth.

Not he that once was great,
swelling with daring, challenging all comers,

shall even be spoken of, for he is of the past.
And he that came after him   170
has had his three falls wrestling,
and is gone.
But whoever sings to Zeus
the victory song from a full heart,
he shall win all that his heart desires.

Zeus it is that has made man's road;
he it is who has laid down the rule
that understanding comes through suffering.
Instead of sleep, there drips before the heart
the recollected sorrow of past pain.
It is against our wills that we become wise.   180
Forced indeed upon us is the grace of our gods
that sit on their solemn thrones.

So on that day, the old leader of the Greek ships,
faulting no prophet, caught his breath at his sudden calamity,
when the Greek host was burdened
with ships halted and empty holds,
as they held the coast over against Chalcis,
at Aulis where the tides roar to and fro.

The hurricane that came from Strymon,   190
breeding deadly delays, starvation, lost anchorages,
driving crews to aimless wanderings,
sparing neither ships nor cables,
wore down the flower of the Argives,
doubling their time with enforced lingering.
So when the prophet's voice rang out,   200
proclaiming to the princes another cure for the bitter storm,
a cure yet heavier to bear,
he backed his prophecies with Artemis's name,
and the twin sons of Atreus beat the ground with their staves

and could not hold back their tears.
Then the old king spoke and said,   210
"Heavy indeed my fate if I disobey,
but heavy, too, if I must butcher my child,
the glory of my house, polluting a father's hands
with streams of a virgin's blood beside the altar.
Which of these two things is without evil?
How shall I become a deserter of my fleet and fail my allies?
There is sacred law on their side, that they passionately covet
a virgin's blood as sacrifice to quell the winds.
May it turn out well."

When he put on the harness of Necessity,   220
his spirit veered in a breath of change—
to impiety, to unholiness, to desecration,
and from it he drew audacity for his heart
to stop at nothing.
For indeed there is a wretched distraction of the wits,
a primal source of ruin,
that puts recklessness in man's mind
and counsels ugliness.
So he dared to become his daughter's sacrificer
to aid the war waged for a woman—
first rites of deliverance for the ships.
Her prayers, and her cries of "Father," and her maiden life   230
they set at nothing, those military umpires.
Her father ordered his servants to lift her
carefully over the altar
after the prayer, swooning, her clothes all round her,
like a young goat,
and with a gag on her beautiful lips
to restrain the cry that would curse his house.
Constrained to voicelessness by the violence of the bit,   240
she slipped to the ground her saffron robes,
and with darting, pitiful eyes struck each of her sacrificers.

She stood out, like a figure in a picture, struggling to speak,
for often she had sung in her father's hospitable halls,
and with pure maiden voice lovingly honored
her beloved father's victory hymn,
with its triple libation to bring good luck.
What happened after that I neither saw nor tell.   250
But Calchas's divining art bore fruit;
the scales of justice have come down and brought,
with suffering, understanding.
You will learn the future when it happens.
Till then, let it be.
To do otherwise is to have sorrow before you need.
For it will come clear with the dawn's light.

                                    (*Enter Clytemnestra.*)

But at the end of all this let there be good fortune.
Surely that is the wish of this (*turning to the queen*)
our sole and closest bulwark against trouble in Argos.
I have come, Queen Clytemnestra, to pay you my respects;   260
for it is right, in the absence of the prince,
to honor the wife of the man whose throne is empty.
I would be glad to know
if you are sure of good tidings or not.
Is it in the hope of happy news
that you are ordering sacrifice?
But I won't resent it if you must be silent.

Clytemnestra
    As the proverb goes,
    "May dawn be the dawn of good news
    as she comes from her mother night"—
    you shall learn of a joy greater than you hope.
    For the Argives have captured Priam's city.
Chorus
    What? I cannot believe you; I cannot understand.
Clytemnestra
    Troy is the Greeks' city now. Are my words clear?

Chorus

Joy steals over me, and calls out tears, too.   270

Clytemnestra

Your eyes proclaim you a subject true and loyal.

Chorus

What makes you trust the news? Have you proof of it?

Clytemnestra

I have, of course—unless the gods deceived me.

Chorus

Dream visions? Do you believe in them?

Clytemnestra

No sleeping mind for me, no, nor its fancies.

Chorus

Have flying rumors bloated you?

Clytemnestra

As if I were a child, you taunt me.

Chorus

But when was it that the city was sacked?

Clytemnestra

In this last night that brought this dawn to birth.

Chorus

What messenger can be as quick as that?   280

Clytemnestra

The god of fire, sending his brilliant glow from Mount Ida.
Beacon sent beacon here with courier fires,
Ida to the crag of Hermes in Lemnos;
then from that island a third flame sent on
was welcomed by the heights of Athos that belong to Zeus;
and high, spanning the sea's back,
the strength of the escorting flame went joyously onward.
The pine fire sent its golden blaze, almost a sun,
to the watchtowers of Macistus.
He didn't hesitate nor carelessly succumb to sleep,   290
but passed his share of the message,
and from afar, over the streams of Euripus,
he gave to the sentries of Messapion

the sign that the beacon's light had traveled to him.
They in their turn lit up and sent the message farther,
firing a great heap of ancient gorse.
Still strong, the beacon's light never flagged,
but leapt over the plain of Asopus like a radiant moon,
to Mount Cithaeron, and there awakened
another relay of traveling fire.
The guard station did not refuse the far-escorted flame;   300
it kindled more than was ordered, and launched its light
over the Gorgon lake; and coming to
the goat-haunted mountain,
urged the watchman not to scant the ordinance of fire.
They lit a huge beard of flame that burnt ungrudgingly,
and sent it over the Saronic gulf, now become its mirror,
beyond the headland, till it struck the heights of Arachnus,
our neighboring sentry post here, and then again
struck right here on this roof of the sons of Atreus—
this fire that is the grandchild of that fire on Mount Ida.
Such were the courses of the torchbearers,   310
one from the other in relays,
and victor is he that ran first and last.
Such proof I have and such confirmation,
sent me out of Troy by my man.

Chorus

My lady, to the gods once again
I shall give my prayer of thanks,
but I would like you to tell me all this again,
that I might hear the words and marvel at them
from beginning to end.

Clytemnestra

Troy is captured; this is the day; the Greeks hold it.   320
Within that city there rings out
a volume of cries that do not mingle.
This is how I see it.
Mix oil and vinegar in the same jar
and you could not call them friends;

they will not be at one.
So in Troy you might hear two sorts of crying:
the conquered and the conquerors.
\\The act is single, the meaning double.
Here are these:
throwing themselves on the dead bodies
of husbands and brothers,
children on the bodies of their fathers,
all sorrowing for the destiny of their dead,
they cry from throats no longer free.
Then there are the others: 330
roving all night after the fight
sets them down hungry to breakfast
on such foods as the city has;
they all share, no rank or place assigned,
but as each has got the luck of the draw.
They are already living in Troy's captured houses,
free of the frost beneath the sky, free of the dews.
They will sleep all night long without a guard,
like happy men.
If they revere the gods of that city in that captured land,
if they revere the gods' sacred places,
they who are conquerors will not be reconquered.
Only let no lust seize the army first,   340
let no greed conquer them,
to make them ravish what they should not.
They must still make the home voyage safely,
travel the other leg of the double track.
But even if the army came through offenseless
in the sight of the gods,
the wrong done to the dead may yet awaken,
seeking to contrive some sudden mishief.
This is what you hear from me, a woman.
But may the good prevail for all to see, past dispute.
Of the many good things I might have,
this is what I would choose.

Chorus

My lady, you talk wisely, like a sensible man.   350
I have learned from you your convincing proofs,
and now again I prepare to greet the gods.
Surely we should thank them for what they have done for us.
O Zeus the king, and friendly night,
that has endowed us with great glory,
you that have cast upon the towers of Troy
a close-fitting mesh so that no one young or old
can overleap the great net of slavery,
the all-catching trap of ruin—
great Zeus of guest-friends I revere.
He has done all this. He has forever bent his bow   360
against Alexander, that no bolt should fail,
neither missing the mark not scaling the stars.
They can say, "It is the stroke of Zeus";
the track of it is clear to see.
Zeus has acted as he has determined.
Someone has said,   370
"The gods do not deign to take heed of mortals
who trample underfoot the grace of holiness."
But he that said that had no piety in him.
The recklessness stands revealed
of those who breathe war beyond justice.
It is a recklessness that breeds consequences
when houses are overcrammed
beyond the measure of the best.
So I escape harm, let but a sufficiency be mine,   380
with abundance of good judgment.
For wealth gives no defense
for the man insolent with gorging,
who kicks the great altar of justice
to where none can see it.
Wretched persuasion,
intolerable child of forecounseling ruin,
drives him on violently.

And all cure is vain. It is not hidden, no—
the mischief shines, a lamp of evil light.
The black grain in Paris shows through the test,   390
like base copper rubbed bare with use.
He has been like a child that chases a bird;
he has brought on this city an intolerable infection,
and no one of the gods will hear his prayer—
rather, pull down the unjust man
conversant with such things.
Such a one is Paris, who came
to the house of the sons of Atreus
and stained with shame the table of his host
by the theft of that host's wife.
She has left to her fellow citizens   400
the clanging of shields, the arming of sailors, ambushes.
To Ilium she has brought ruin instead of dowry.
Her daring defying all limits,
she darted quickly through the gates.
And many a groan there was
among those that spoke for the palace:
"Ah me, ah me, for the house, the house and the princes.   410
Ah me for the bed and the tracks of the love of men on it."
There one can see the silence—
dishonored, unreviling, inexorable—
of him that sits apart.
Through yearning for the one gone over the sea,
a ghost will seem to rule the house.
The grace of beautiful statues is hateful to the man.
Their eyes are empty, and before them
all passionate love falls dead.
Fancies haunt him in dreams persuasively;   420
theirs is a grace without substance.
Unsubstantial it is, when one sees,
and dreaming reaches to the touch,
and the phantom is gone, quickly slipping through his hands,
as it follows the winged paths of sleep.

Such are the sorrows at home at the hearth;
but there are worse than these for all,
for those who joined the fleet and left the land of Greece.
In the house of every one of these   430
preeminent there is grief that reaches the heart.
They know whom they have sent forth, but instead of men
there come home urns and ashes to each house.
The war god is a money changer;
men's bodies are his money.
He holds the scales in the battle of the spear.
From Ilium he sends back to those who loved them   440
the scrapings of dust made heavy with their tears;
he loads the elegant urns with the dust that was once a man.
They mourn this man as they praise him—
how skilled he was in the fight—and another—
how gallantly he fell in his blood—
for another man's woman.
That is what they whisper and snarl;   450
and pain creeps about, full of ill will
toward the plaintiffs, the sons of Atreus.
But those others keep to their graves in all their beauty,
where they were, around the walls of Troy.
The enemy land that they have taken at last
has taken them, hidden them in itself.
The malicious speech of citizens is hard to bear;
it is the equal of a public curse.
And still I am troubled, lest I come to hear   460
something hidden in dark night.

For watchful are the gods' eyes
for those that kill by the thousands.
The black Furies reduce to dim nothingness
the man whose success has no justice in it,
wear him down, reversing his life's fortune.
And when he is among those we cannot see,

there is no help for him.
To be too well spoken of is heavy indeed.
For the thunderbolt is hurled from the eyes of Zeus.   470
May I not be a city-sacker, nor yet look upon my own life,
captured by others.
Swift is the rumor coursing through the city,
spurred by the fire of good tidings.
But whether it is true, who knows, or whether
somehow the gods deceive us.
Who is there so childish, so maimed of wit,   480
that the messages of fire should kindle his heart
only to sicken later when the news changes?
It is like the mettle of a woman's spirit
to praise the gracious gift before it is certainly there.
The limits of a woman's belief can be
as easily and quickly crossed
as cattle graze across a boundary.
But quickly, too, dies the report
a woman utters.
Soon we shall know about the lights from the beacons   490
and all the exchange of watch fires:
whether they are true or whether, like dreams,
a light of joy has stolen upon us and cheated our minds.
Here I see the herald coming from the shore,
shaded with twigs of olive.
The thirsty dust, twin sister of mud across the boundary,
is my witness; it witnesses to me that he has a *real* voice,
and so his testimony is not one of the smoky fire
of some wood on the hillside.
He will rather speak out and tell us to be glad,
or—God forbid it is the contrary message.
There *have* been good things that have shown through;
grant that this is their consummation.
Whoever prays anything else for this city,   500
I would he might reap the fruit of his mistaken thoughts.

(Enter a herald.)

Herald

   O my fathers' earth, Argos, Argos,
ten long years and I have come to you;
so many shipwrecked hopes, and one a winner.
I never dreamed that I would have for my share in death
a piece of dearest Argive land.
Now welcome earth, welcome the light of sun,
and Zeus supreme lord; and the Pythian King,
no longer shooting his arrows against us;
you were harsh enough along Scamander's banks,   510
but now you are different, now you are savior and healer,
King Apollo. My greetings to all the gods in assembly.
My greeting to my patron god, Hermes, dear herald,
whom all heralds worship.
My greetings to the heroes that sent us out
and kindly welcome back what's left of us after the fight.
Hail, royal halls, roofs I have loved,
hail, holy seats and you divinities that face the sunlight.
Receive now with faces bright in joy—   520
if ever you did in days gone by—
now receive the king in glory after so long.
He comes and brings light after night's darkness,
a light to you and to all these—
King Agamemnon.
Give him true welcome; truly it belongs to him,
the king who dug down Troy with the spade of God's justice,
made plowland of Troy;
and the seed has perished from all their country.
Their altars and the shrines of their gods are gone.   530
Such a yoking chain has he cast on Troy,
the king, Atreus's son, the old and happy man.
And now he comes here, most worthy of all
that now live and die.
Neither Paris nor the city that supports him
can boast that they have done more than they have paid for.

He was condemned for rape and theft—
lost what he carried off.
He has reaped for harvest
the utter ruin of his father's house.
And doubly have the sons of Priam paid for their offenses.
Chorus
Herald of the Argive army, joy on your homecoming!
Herald
Joy, indeed. If the gods should end my life now,
I'd not deny them.
Chorus
Has the love of your lost homeland tortured you so?   540
Herald
Yes; the tears you see are tears of joy.
Chorus
That disease had its pleasure for you, all the same.
Herald
What disease? What should I understand by that?
Chorus
Love's stroke. But you got love for the love you gave.
Herald
You mean this land has missed the army as we missed you?
Chorus
We were faint and weak and so have groaned for you.
Herald
Why so uneasy? What horror was in your mind?
Chorus
I say nothing and am safe—a long, long silence.
Herald
How could that be? Your king was away; did you fear others?
Chorus
As you said just now, I would have welcomed death.   550
Herald
It *has* been a success. Of course, in the length of time,
one must say some things have gone well, some ill.
Who except the gods lives the whole span of his life

without trouble?
Yes, if I were to speak of the hard work
and the bad quarters,
the narrow gangways and the hard beds,
there's plenty to complain about.
Then there were the troubles on land,
disgusting things, too.
Our beds were under the enemy's walls.
Rain from the sky and dew from the grass soaked us   560
and kept rotting our clothing
and bred lice in our hair.
I could talk about the winter, which killed the birds;
Mount Ida and its snow made that intolerable.
And then there was the heat,
when the sea fell on its noontide bed and slept.
Not a breath of wind, not a stir on the waves—
Oh, why should I still feel pain for all this?
It's over, isn't it, all the trouble?
It's over indeed, for them, too, the dead;
they'll never have to trouble about getting up again.
Why should I reckon up the numbers of those who are gone?   570
Why should the living grieve because
fortune turned against us?
I'm ready to say a long goodbye to all that's happened.
For us that are left of the Greek army,
the gain certainly wins out,
and the bad side of things doesn't weigh it down.
So, those of us who have sped over land and sea
can stand facing the sunlight and make our boast:
"There was a day when the Argive army took Troy.
They have nailed the spoils of it
on the homes of the gods throughout Greece
to be a glory forever and ever."
When they hear this, men must praise   580
the city and its generals.
We shall also honor the grace of God

who brought it to pass.
That's my whole speech.

Chorus

What you say wins me over; I admit it.
To be ready to learn is what makes a young man
out of an old one.
But it is this house and Clytemnestra
that the news most concerns,
though I, too, am the richer for it.

Clytemnestra

I rejoiced long ago,
and raised the cry of joy over the news,
when first the fire came as my messenger in the night,
telling of Troy's capture and destruction.
That was when everyone found fault with me: 590
"Is it beacon fires that convince you
that Troÿ has now been sacked?
How like a woman's heart to be so lifted up."
In rumors such as these I appeared
to have gone astray in my wits.
But yet I made the sacrifices,
and following this "woman's fashion"
they all raised the chant, now here, now there,
throughout the city,
the songs of blessing at the gods' shrines,
and there they lulled to sleep
the sweet-smelling sacrificial fires.
Why *now* should I depend on you to tell me more?
I shall learn the whole story from my lord himself.
How shall I make best haste to receive him home,   600
my honored husband?
What sweeter day for a wife's eye to see
than when she opens the doors to her man
coming from the army,
when the gods have brought him safely back to her?

Tell my husband this:
bid him come as quick as he can,
the city's darling.
And when he comes may he find his wife
true as he left her,
the watchdog of his house,
devoted to him, enemy to his enemies,
the same always and ever.
I never broke the seal   610
in all those years.
I know of no pleasure with another man
nor any talk or evil gossip against me,
anymore than I know how to dip this blade
to temper it.
Such is my boast, so full of truth
that even a well-bred wife
need not blush to utter it.

                                        (*Exit Clytemnestra.*)

Chorus
    She has spoken very suitably
    for those who understand her.
    But tell me, Herald,
    what of Menelaus?
    Was he among the returning army?
    Is he safe among you?
    And will he come back home again, our dear prince?
Herald
    I don't know how to put a fair face on lies: 620
    my friends would only have good of it
    for a short time anyway.
Chorus
    Why can't you tell news that is both good and true?
    When you separate them, you can't get away with it.
Herald
    Then—the man has vanished from the Greek army,
    he and his ship. *That* is not a lie.

Chorus
> Did you see him set forth from Ilium on his own?
> Or did some storm that struck you all together
> snatch him away?

Herald
> You've hit it exactly;   630
> in a few words you've covered a long, sad story.

Chorus
> What do the rest of his shipmates think?
> Do they say he's alive or dead?

Herald
> No one knows how to tell the news clearly—
> except the sun, there, that gives life to the world.

Chorus
> What do you mean? Was there a storm
> that came upon the fleet by the gods' anger
> and then ended?

Herald
> A day of good news—one should not infect it
> with the tongue of bad news.
> The honor due to the two kinds of gods
> is separate.
> When a messenger with a gloomy face bears cursed news   640
> of an army's downfall,
> there is one common injury which is public,
> and then, besides, many a man is banned from his home;
> this is the double lash that the god of war loves,
> a two-speared ruin, a bloody pair.
> When, I say, a messenger is loaded with such calamities,
> he must sing his news as his hymn to the Furies.
> But when the saving messenger of good news
> comes to a city that rejoices in well-being
> —how should I mingle good with bad
> in telling you of this storm
> which surely did proceed from the gods' anger
> against the Greeks?

For fire and sea, those two oldest and deepest of enemies,   650
swore a conspiracy and pledged their common allegiance
to destroy the wretched Greek army.
In the night, waves lashed by the storm
arose to plague us.
For the Thracian winds battered ship on ship.
Butting one another savagely
in the hurricane and sheets of hail,
they sank from sight, as our evil shepherd
drove us here and there.
When the clear light of the day came back,
we saw the sea blooming,
and its flowers were dead Greeks and wrecks.
For ourselves and our boat, we went unharmed;   660
some god stole us through it or begged us off;
he must have steered us himself,
for no man touched the steering oar.
Luck chose to become our savior, and sat on our ship,
so that we missed the driving waves when we were at anchor,
nor were driven aground on the rugged land.
Afterward, when we had escaped our watery hell,
in the white light of day, we hardly dared to trust our luck;
and in our own thoughts we were constantly
shepherds of some new calamity,
seeing how the fleet had been pounded and ground to pieces.
Now, if any of them still breathes,   670
they speak of us as lost; of course they do.
We have much the same idea about them.
Let it turn out well. For Menelaus,
in all likelihood you may expect him back.
For if the beams of the sun discover him living and seeing,
through the workings of God—
for surely God will not yet blot out
the whole family—
there is some hope that he'll come home again.

This is really the truth that you have heard.   680

                     (Exit herald.)

Chorus
    Who can have named her so,
    with such truth, utterly?
    Could it be someone we cannot see,
    with foreknowledge of destiny,

Chorus
    Who can have named her so,
    with such truth, utterly?
    Could it be someone we cannot see,
    with foreknowledge of destiny,
    that used his tongue in harmony with fortune?
    She was called Helen,
    the bride won by the spear, sought in strife.
    Helen means death, and death indeed she was,   690
    death to ships and men and city
    as she sailed out of the delicate fabrics of her curtained room,
    fanned by the breeze of giant Zephyr;
    and the man-swarm of shield-bearing hunters
    came on the track of her,
    the vanished track of the oar blades
    which beached on the ever-green shores of Simoeis
    on the heels of their bloody quarrel.

    To Ilium it drove her,   700
    the wrath that brings fulfillment,
    and again the word proved true, that equates
    marriage and mourning,
    for the wrath exacted vengeance at the last
    for the guest-table dishonored at the hearth shared by Zeus.
    Wrath punished as victims those men,
    the new marriage kinsmen,
    who on that day must celebrate,
    sing out of full throats
    the hymn that honored the bride.

Perhaps that ancient city of Priam   710
has learned another tune now,
a tuneful dirge that calls him
Paris the dismally bedded;
the city has endured the ruin of its life,
the voice of countless lamentations,
through the wretched bloodletting of its citizens.
Once on a time there was a man
who raised a lion cub in his home.
It was a little thing, starved of milk,   720
still a suckling, still in the first rituals of its life,
gentle, a friend of children,
and a delight to the old.
Many a time it lay in their arms,
like a young baby;
its face was bright as it fawned on the hand
at the dictates of its belly's needs.
But time passed, and it showed
what disposition it had from its breeding;
it requited the grace of those that brought it up
by horrid slaughtering of their sheep,
an unbidden dinner guest.
And the house was confused and befouled with blood;   730
an evil it was that the servants couldn't fight,
a very murderous mischief.
God reared the lion in the house to become
an additional priest of ruin.
But on that first day—as I tell the story—
she came to the city of Ilium
a spirit of windless calm,
the delicate glory of wealth,
the soft arrow darting from her eyes,
the flower of love that bites the heart.
Then she changed direction, and brought   740
a bitter ending to the marriage,
hastening to the daughters of Priam

to sit with them and live with them
to their ruin.
Zeus, the god of guests, brought her there,
a Fury to make wives weep.
There is an old saying among men, first spoken long ago,   750
that a man's great prosperity, when perfected,
gives birth and doesn't die childless,
but from that good fortune in true descent
there grows an ever-greedy misery.
In this, my mind is different from others'.
No, I say, it is the wicked deed
that breeds more wickedness, and like to its own kind.
For the house that is straight-dealing and just   760
is fated always to have good children.
The ancient deed of sacrilege always breeds a young one,
full of disaster for man, now or then,
when comes the dawn appointed for its birth.
A spirit but a clansman—
one cannot war against him nor fight him—
he is a thing unholy,
a daring, a black ruin to the halls,
and very like his parents.
For justice shines in houses grimed with smoke,   770
and she honors the good man.
And those gilded palaces where hands are dirty
she leaves, averting her eyes;
she goes to what is clean,
for she doesn't honor power
whose coinage is misstamped by the praise of the rich.
And she guides everything to its due end.   780
                    (*Enter Agamemnon and Cassandra.*)
My lord, conqueror of Troy, descendant of Atreus,
how shall I greet you, how do you reverence,
neither exceeding nor scanting due measure of praise?
Many men, indeed, who transgress justice,
honor appearance over reality.

Everyone is ready to cry over the unfortunate,   790
but the bite of that sorrow doesn't reach the heart.
So, too, there are those that seem to share joy,
yet the faces that they force have no laughter in them.
When one is a good judge of stock,
one doesn't miss the meaning of the man's eyes,
fawning in watery friendship
when they seem all loyalty.
In the days when you led the expedition from Greece,   800
for Helen's sake,
I saw you painted in ugly colors—
I will not hide that from you—
as one who had an unskillful hand
on the rudder of his wits
when you tried to win back through men's dying
a willing whore.
But now from the depth of my heart, in true friendship,
I say, May the work be kind to those who did it so well.
In time you shall know by enquiry
which of your citizens that stayed here at home
dealt justly, and which did wrong.

Agamemnon

First Argos and my country's gods,   810
I must address you; you and I are coauthors
of my home return and the justice
I exacted from Priam's city.
The causes were not spoken aloud,
but the gods heard them
and cast their votes with no opposing voices
into the bloody urn: for Ilium's destruction
and the deaths of men.
To the other urn nothing drew near
but the shadowy hope of a hand;
there was no filling that urn.
You can still see the smoke from the city's capture.
The hot blasts of ruin live there yet,

60

but there is ash, too, dying
as it sends into the air its breaths fattened on rich things.
For all of this we should pay our gods   820
much-remembering thanks.
We have taken vengeance for insolent robbery.
And for the sake of a woman a city has been leveled
by the biting beast of Argos, the colt,
the shield-bearing host,
that made its leap about the time of the setting Pleiades.
A ravening lion leaped over the wall
and licked its fill of royal blood.
So far my prelude stretches; that's for the gods.
What you've said of your feelings, I've heard and remember.   830
I say the same. You have me as your advocate.
In very few men is it native
to admire a successful friend without envying him.
For the poison of malice, settling on the heart,
doubles its weight in one who is stricken with envy.
He suffers under the load of his own troubles,
and groans to see the prosperity of the other man.
I know of what I speak; I very well understand
the glassy mirror of comradeship, that shadow of a shade,
which those prove to be who seemed my truest friends.
Only Odysseus, who joined the fleet unwillingly,   840
once he was yoked was for me a ready trace horse.
Even as I speak of him, I do not know
if I speak of the dead or the living.
For other matters, we will set up public meetings
and take counsel in full assembly.
What is now well shall remain well; we shall see to it.
But where there is need for healing medicines,
we will try by surgery or cautery
intelligently to avert the disease.
Now I will go in, into my halls, my hearth, my home,   850
and there I will first greet the gods
who sent me forth and brought me back again.

Victory has followed us;
let her be ours still, constantly!

(*Enter Clytemnestra.*)

Clytemnestra
　　You citizens, elders of Argos,
　　I will not be ashamed of speaking to you
　　of how I love my husband.
　　Modest inhibition is something
　　that dies away in human dealings.
　　I will tell of how wretched my life has been
　　while this man was in Troy—
　　at first hand I will tell it; it has been *my* life.
　　First, that a woman should sit in her house,　　　　　　　860
　　lonely without her male,
　　is something terrifying.
　　She hears so many hateful rumors;
　　here's one has come, and then another,
　　announcing a greater disaster still,
　　mouthing the ruin of the house.
　　If this man here had had as many wounds
　　as streams of rumor would have it,
　　he would have had more holes in him than a net.
　　If he had died, as his deaths multiplied in stories of him,　870
　　he must have had three bodies, like Geryon;
　　he would have boasted of taking a triple
　　shroud of earth to himself.
　　It was because of these hateful reports
　　that others, not I, have loosened many a cord
　　as it tightened round my neck.
　　And that is why your son
　　doesn't stand beside me as he should,
　　the proof of our trust, mine to you, yours to me,
　　our Orestes.
　　Do not wonder at this; a loyal ally keeps him safe,　　　880
　　Strophius the Phocian.
　　He spoke to me of twin troubles:

your danger at Ilium, and then that here, too,
the anarchy of the people's voices
might overturn good counsel.
Indeed, it is inbred in men
to kick the man that's down.
That's the advice of Strophius, and there's no deceit in it.
For my own part, the gushing springs of my grief
have dried up;
there's not a drop left.
My eyes are in pain from late watching,
weeping for the beacons that should tell of you,
but never called for firing.
In my dreams, I have started up,   890
roused by the light strokes of the gnat's flight;
I have seen so much more happen to you
than could be contained within the time
with which I shared my sleep.
But now I have come through all this;
my heart is free of sorrow;
and so I can describe this man of mine—
a watchdog of the house,
the saving forestay of the ship,
the rooted pillar of the towering roof,
the single child of a father,
the land seen by sailors when they had given over hope,
the fairest day to see after the storm,   900
the springwater stream for the thirsty traveler.
It is sweet indeed to escape the harsh stroke of necessity.
Such terms of address would, I think, belong to him.
But let no one be jealous.
Many, indeed, were the evils we endured before.
Now, dear heart,
step from the carriage, but do not place on earth, my king,
this foot that trod Troy to destruction.
Servants, to whom I have commanded the task
of strewing his path to the house with tapestries—

hubris

let his way lie straight before him strewn with purple,   910
that justice may guide him to the home he never hoped for.
Everything else earned by fate
an unsleeping mind, with the help of the gods,
will arrange justly.

Agamemnon

Daughter of Leda, guardian of my house,
your speech is a good fit for my absence:
both have stretched out long.
But to praise me in due fashion
is an honor that others should give.
Besides, do not make much of me in this woman's fashion,
nor grovel and gape flatteringly, like some foreigner,
nor strew my path with garments that would make it
an object of ill will;
it is the gods one should honor with such things.   920
For one who is mortal, for me certainly,
to walk on subtly woven beauties like these
cannot be without fear.
I tell you, honor me as man, not god.
Footmats and embroideries—they sound differently,
they are different.
Not to be presumptuous
is the greatest gift the gods can give you.
It's only when a life has ended, and ended well,
that one dare say, "Well done."
I would be cheerful if my life   930
were like this in everything.

Clytemnestra

Then tell me this, and let it be your own true judgment.

Agamemnon

Be sure, I will not falsify that judgment.

Clytemnestra

Was it through fear of the gods
that you made this vow?

Agamemnon
I said, if any man ever did, what I knew would happen.
Clytemnestra
And what of Priam, if he had conquered as you have?
Agamemnon
He would certainly have trodden on the tapestry.
Clytemnestra
Don't be ashamed, then, of human reproach.
Agamemnon
Yes, but the ill repute of the people's voices
has a great power.
Clytemnestra
He that is not envied is also not admired.
Agamemnon
A woman should not long so for a fight.   940
Clytemnestra
In those that win, yielding is graceful.
Agamemnon
Do you set such store on victory in this dispute?
Clytemnestra
Let me have my way. You are the victor
if you yield readily.
Agamemnon
Well, if you will—here, someone undo my sandals,
that are like slaves for the treading of my foot.
And as I walk upon these lovely cloths,
I pray against the envious eye of the gods
lest from afar it strike me.
It's a great shame to spoil a house's wealth,
these weavings so dear in price, with the dirt of treading feet.
Enough of this.   950
Bring in this stranger here, and use her kindly.
The god looks from afar with approval
on the merciful conqueror.
No one chooses to become a slave.

This woman is the very flower, picked out
from the spoils of war;
as a gift from the army to me, she followed me.
Well, since I've been subdued to listen to you,
I will go into my house, treading on purple.

Clytemnestra

There is a sea—and who shall drain it dry?—
nourishing a spring, always new, an abundance of purple
to be bought with silver for the dyeing of garments.
This house, my lord, has store enough of it,   960
thanks be to the gods.
This house does not know poverty.
I would have vowed the treading of many garments,
had I been so ordered by the shrines of the oracles,
to win the safe return of your life.
When the root is there, the leaf comes to the house,
and stretches its shade against the dog star's heat.
And when you came to this house and hearth of yours,
it meant what heat means in the winter time.
And when Zeus makes wine from the bitter grape,   970
it is still cool within the house,
when its perfected lord paces through the halls.
Zeus, Zeus, that brings all to perfection,
perfect my prayer.
Bring to perfection all you have to do.

Chorus

Why this fluttering, insistent terror
that keeps guard before my heart?
Is the song prophetic   980
that rises unhired and unbidden?
My grounded mind has no confidence to dismiss it
like an obscure nightmare.
Time has grown old since the boats,
their hawsers all thrown out along the sands,
set out to Ilium.

With my eyes I am my own witness
to their homecoming.
But nonetheless, my spirit within me   990
drones this tune of the Furies,
accompanied by no lyre,
a song taught by none but itself.
It has none of the dear confidence of hope.
Not for nothing is the boding of my entrails,
the whirling of my heart, harmonized with
eddies of my mind that will surely bring fulfillment.
But I pray that what I expect may fall away,
a lie, into unfulfillment.
There is no limit in health;   1000
it is insatiable.
For disease is its next-door neighbor;
there is but a single wall between them.
A man's destiny, facing straight ahead,
often crashes on the hidden reef.
Yet, if beforehand in prudent fear,
he casts overboard part of what he owns
with the derrick of good measure,
his whole house does not sink utterly,   1010
though overloaded to overflowing,
nor does the frame of the ship sink.
Many times the generous gifts of Zeus,
and those of the furrows yearly tilled,
banish the disease of hunger.
But the black blood of a man,   1020
when once it has fallen to the earth in his death,
who shall conjure it back again with any incantation?
Did not Zeus, for the safety of the world,
stop the wizard who would raise the dead?
If there were no fates appointed by the gods
which checked other fates from having overmuch,
my heart would have outstripped my tongue
and poured this out.

But now in the dark it mutters, in heart-anguish,   1030
with never a hope of spinning out of my burning mind
what is right for this moment.

Clytemnestra

In with you too, now, Cassandra,
since Zeus (you cannot be angry with Zeus)
has made you a sharer in the sacrifices in our house,
standing near the altar with many slaves that we own.
Get down from that carriage;
none of your high spirit of pride.
They say that Heracles, Alcmenes' son,   1040
was sold and forced to eat the bread of slavery.
If then the necessity of fate's scales
has forced this on you,
you should be very grateful for masters anciently rich.
Those who have reaped a harvest they never expected
are always excessive in harshness toward their slaves.
From us you will have all the usual treatment.

Chorus

She has finished; it is to you she spoke,
and what she says is clear enough.
You are taken, a quarry in fate's net;
obey her, then—
though I will understand if you don't.

Clytemnestra

If she has anything besides her swallow twitterings,   1050
a barbaric speech that no one knows,
I'll try to persuade her within her understanding.

Chorus

Follow her. What she says is the best there is for you;
leave the carriage; obey her.

Clytemnestra

I have no time to waste here with her
outside the palace.
The sheep stand ready for slaughter

in front of the hearth at the center of the house.

(*To Cassandra.*)

You, if you're going to do anything that I tell you,
do it quickly.
But if you disobey because you don't take in my words—

(*To Chorus.*)

Here, you!
Don't speak to her any more; use your hands;
that's all these foreigners understand.

Chorus

I think the woman needs a good interpreter;   1060
she looks like a wild thing newly caught.

Clytemnestra

She's crazy; she hears only her distraught mind.
Of course she does, she that has left her newly captured city,
come here not yet knowing how to wear the curb bit,
till she's frothed out her spirit in blood.
I won't throw any more words at her to be belittled.

(*Exit Clytemnestra.*)

Chorus

I pity her, and so I won't be angry.   1070
Come, you poor girl, desert your place in the carriage;
yield to what must be; wear your yoke for the first time.

Cassandra

Oh! Oh! Oh! Oh, the land!
Lord Apollo! Lord Apollo!

Chorus

Why do you raise such dismal cries to Apollo?
He is no god for the singer of dirges.

Cassandra

Oh! Oh! Oh! Oh, the land!
Lord Apollo! Lord Apollo!

Chorus

Again she calls with her ill omens
upon the god who has no suitable place
at scenes of mourning.

She will take him in the folds of the robe
with the trick of the black horn.
She strikes! He falls! He falls
in the water of the bath.

Cassandra

Lord Apollo! Lord Apollo! God of the streets,   1080
god of destruction! Now again, god of my destruction,
and so easily.

Chorus

She seems to me about to prophesy her own misfortunes.
The gift of prophecy still sticks
even though the mind is now a slave's.

Cassandra

Lord Apollo! Lord Apollo!
God of my destruction! God of the streets!
Through what streets have you led me now,
to what house?

Chorus

To that of the sons of Atreus. If you don't know that,
that I can tell you. And you won't say it's a lie.

Cassandra

Yes, to a house the gods hate;   1090
it has been witness of so many
murders of kin, butcheries,
bowl full of man's blood, ground soaked in shed blood.

Chorus

The stranger has a nose as keen as a hound;
she's on the trail of a murder and will find it.

Cassandra

What convinces me are the witnesses—
the children, the babies screaming of their cut throats,
of their flesh roasted and eaten by their father.

Chorus

We have heard of your fame as a prophet;
but we need no foretellers here.

Cassandra

Oh, what does she plan? 1100
What is the great new grief?
It is a great evil against the house
that she is planning.
It is unbearable for its friends, uncurable.
Defense stands aloof and keeps away.

Chorus

These last foretellings are quite beyond my understanding;
the others I know—indeed the whole city cries them aloud.

Cassandra

Oh, you wretched woman,
is this what you bring to consummation?
You have cleaned him in the bath
till his skin shined,
the husband to share your bed.
And how shall I tell the consummation?
It would be quick: the line of clutching hands, 1110
stretching out, one hooked to another.

Chorus

I don't understand that yet;
you spoke riddles before,
but now what baffles me is the dimness
of what comes from the gods in words.

Cassandra

Oh! Oh! Oh! What is this that appears?
A net, a net of death. Can it be so?
But the meshes are the bedfellow, the accomplice in murder.
Let the pack that ravens insatiate against the family
bay for a sacrifice that merits death by stoning.

Chorus

What Fury is this you bid raise its cries
against the house?
I find no cleaning in your words. 1120
To my heart rush back the blood drops of yellowing stain,
as when the eyes grow dim at the setting of a life's day,

a man falling by the point of a spear.
And destruction comes quick.

Cassandra

Look at that! Look at that!
Keep away the bull from the cow!
That is his end, I tell you,
a treacherous murder in a cauldron.

Chorus

I will not boast of being a keen judge of prophecy,   1130
but this certainly looks like something evil.
Anyway, what good word ever came to mankind
from the prophets?
It is through evils that the wordy tricks of the prophets
bring terrors for us to understand.

Cassandra

Oh, the ill boding of my own sad fate!
For it is my own suffering, on top of his,
that my tongue spills out.

        (*To the god.*)

Where is this you have brought me to in my sorrow?
For nothing but to share his death; what else?

Chorus

You are someone god-possessed;   1140
the god carries you along.
It is for yourself you cry out this tuneless tune.
Like the brown nightingale, that can never have
enough of song,
as she cries "Itys! Itys!" for her life rich in sorrows,
and her mind loves pity for herself.

Cassandra

Oh! The life of the shrill-voiced nightingale!
The gods covered *her* with a feathered body;
I tell you, they gave her a *sweet* life,
and her cries are not cries of sorrow.
But what remains for me
is the splitting of the flesh with the two-edged spear.

Chorus

> Where do they come from, these rushes 1150
> of useless agony carried by the god?
> You make music that is a mixture,
> ugly cries of terror and high-pitched melodies.
> Where did you get the milestones of evil words
> that mark your prophetic journey?

Cassandra

> The marriage! The marriage of Paris,
> deadly to those who loved him.
> Scamander, river that my fathers drank of,
> in that time I was raised on your shores;
> but now around the banks of Cocytus and Acheron, 1160
> the rivers of death, I am likely to prophesy,
> and soon.

Chorus

> What is this word you have spoken all too clearly?
> A newborn child could understand.
> The bite of murder has pierced me
> as you whimper at your painful fortune.
> It is a heartbreak to hear you.

Cassandra

> The agony, agony of the city utterly ruined.
> The sacrifices that my father made before the walls,
> the multiplied slaughter of cattle and woolly sheep.
> None of it helped; it was no cure. 1170
> The city suffered as it was fated to suffer.
> And I shall soon be thrown on the ground
> in my own warm blood.

Chorus

> What you say now follows what you said before.
> Some malevolent god who falls on you with fearful weight
> makes you a singer of these deadly mournful things.
> But as for the end—I am at a loss.

Cassandra

> Now my prophecy shall no longer peer from behind veils

like a newly married bride.
No, it will rush on, a wind brightly blowing   1180
into the sun's rising,
to send disaster surging like a wave to meet the sunbeams,
a disaster yet greater than this.
I will not school you in riddles any longer.
And do you be my witness that my nose is keen
and my tracking by shortcuts
on the path of crimes committed long ago.
Never do they leave the house,
that chorus that sings in ugly harmony.
For their speech is of evil.
The revelers have drunk, to whet their courage more,
man's blood, and so they abide in the house,
and none shall expel them: they are the Furies,
that attend on the murder of kin.
The song they sing as they beleaguer the house   1190
is the song of the primal destruction,
when the mind is blinded.
And each of the Furies has spat in disgust
on the brother's bed that hates its violator.
Hah! Am I an archer that missed,
or have I hit the mark?
Or am I a false prophet
that raps on doors and babbles?
Be my witness, you, but first make your sworn oath
that I know the story of the ancient sins
of this house.
Chorus
How would such an oath, even plighted in all honesty,
serve as any kind of cure?
True, I do wonder at you,   1200
that you, reared beyond the sea and speaking a strange tongue
should talk of these things as if you had been there.
Cassandra
It was Apollo the prophet

that charged me with the office of prophecy.

Chorus

He fell in love with you?

Is that possible for a god?

Cassandra

Till now I was ashamed to speak of it.

Chorus

As long as things go well, one has one's delicacy.

Cassandra

He was a wrestler, that breathed his grace into me.

Chorus

Did you come to the breeding of children,

like other couples?

Cassandra

I promised the god and cheated him.

Chorus

Had you already got your gift of prophecy?

Cassandra

Oh yes, I used to tell my countrymen

all that would happen.   1210

Chorus

How did you escape the god's anger?

Cassandra

Since my offense against him,

no one believed a word of mine.

Chorus

Ah, but to us right now, you seem to prophesy truly.

Cassandra

Oh, oh, my agony! There it is again!

The fearful pain of true prophecy

that twists me, that drives me wild;

and it is still only prelude.

Look! Look! You see them! The young ones,

sitting on the house like dream phantoms.

They are the likenesses of those children dead and gone,

killed by those they loved;

their hands are full of meat, their own flesh.
You can see it clearly; they carry the pitiful load   1220
of their guts, and their father has tasted them.
I tell you, there is punishment for this,
and someone is plotting it,
a lion, but a coward, that wallows, a housekeeper
in the bed of the returning lord—
O mine, *my* lord—for I must bear the yoke of slavery.
The captain of the ships, the sacker of Ilium,
he knows not what tongue is licking him,
the tongue of the hateful bitch, her ears pricked,
like a secret blind vengeance,
that will work out his evil fate.
So far her daring reaches: 1230
the woman will murder the man.
She is—what shall I call her and be right?
this monstrous, biting creature.
A snake with poison at both ends;
some Scylla living in the rocks, death to sailors;
some murderous, raging mother of hell;
some truceless god of war;
a war she has declared upon her loved ones!
So let her cry her war cry,
whose daring knows no limit,
as at the moment when the battle turns.
Yet she seems to rejoice that he has come safe home.
It is all one to me, if you do not believe any of this;
what difference?
It is to be and will come.   1240
Soon you will stand here and say of me, in pity,
she was too true a prophet.
Chorus
The feast of Thyestes, and the flesh of the children,
I understand and shudder; fear is on me
as I hear the truth, and no mere likenesses.

But for the rest I heard from you,
I have fallen off the course and run wide.
Cassandra
I tell you, you will live to see Agamemnon's death.
Chorus
Wretched girl, hold your tongue in piety.
Cassandra
No, no holy god of healing presides over this story.
Chorus
True, if what you say is so; but God forbid it should be.
Cassandra
You are all for God forbidding;   1250
but their job is killing.
Chorus
What man is he that furnishes this grief?
Cassandra
You have surely fallen astray of my prophecies.
Chorus
Yes, for I do not understand how the plotter
will make his plan work.
Cassandra
Yet I know Greek rather too well.
Chorus
So does the Delphic oracle; but it's hard to understand,
all the same.
Cassandra
Oh! It attacks me like fire!
Oh! Oh! O god! O Lycian Apollo!
There she is, the lioness, two-footed bedfellow of the wolf,
in the absence of the true-bred lion.
She will kill me. Like one that brews a potion,   1260
She will put my reward, too, in the drink.
She cries her glee in triumph, as she whets the knife
for a man, to pay him in murder for bringing me here.
                    (*She starts tearing off her robe and garlands.*)

77

Why should I have these mockeries about me,
this staff, the prophet's garlands round my neck?
Before I die myself, I shall at least destroy you.
Go; you shall be no more. Lie on the ground as you fall.
Thus I requite you.
Enrich some other girl with blinded madness,
some other girl than me.
Look, Apollo himself undoes his prophetess   1270
of her prophetic mantle; he has watched me
laughed to scorn even in this trumpery,
laughed at by friends turned foes,
with never a quiver in the scale—what hollowness!
Ill-treated like a wandering beggar priest,
in misery half-starved to death, I still endured.
But now the prophet has unmade the prophet
and brought me here to meet my chance death.
No father's altar, but a chopping block, waits for me,
to be warmed with my blood as I am butchered,
the preliminary victim. Yet, all the same, I shall not die
dishonored by the gods.
But another will come to take vengeance for me;   1280
he will kill the mother in whom he was seeded,
and will avenge his father.
A wanderer outcast, grown alien to this land,
who will return from exile
to put a coping stone of ruin for those he loved,
for he has sworn a great oath by the gods
that his father's corpse shall bring him home again.
Why do I go on this way, crying, full of self-pity?—
now that I have seen Troy's ruin, as I saw it,
now as Troy's conquerors come off in the god's judgment,
as I see them now.
I will go and face it; I will face my death.   1290
These gates before me here, I call you now by name:
the gates of death.
But I pray that the stroke that reaches me

may be a mortal stroke,
that without struggle, as the blood runs freely,
in easy death I may close these eyes of mine.

Chorus

You are a woman that has suffered much,
and have understood much; and you have said much.
But if you truly know your fate,
why do you walk up to the altar steadfastly,
like an ox?

Cassandra

There is no escape, my friends; the time is full.

Chorus

Yet the latest moment has a special value.   1300

Cassandra

This day has come; there is little I would gain by flight.

Chorus

How courageous and steadfast!

Cassandra

No one who's happy hears these compliments.

Chorus

But death, if fame comes with it,
comes still with grace to those that must die anyway.

Cassandra

I weep for you, father, and for your noble children.

                                   (*She recoils.*)

Chorus

What is it? What is the fear that turns you back?

                                   (*Cassandra shudders.*)

Chorus

What made you shudder?
Is it something in your mind that disgusts you?

Cassandra

The house! It reeks of murder, of dripping blood!

Chorus

What? It's just the blood of sacrificed animals.   1310

Cassandra

No, it is just like the smell of a grave.

Chorus

It is no delicate Syrian incense in the house
that you speak of.

Cassandra

Still—I will go into the house,
to mourn with cries my own and Agamemnon's deaths.
I have enough of life.
My friends, I'm not scared
like a bird startled at a bush
in empty terror.
When I die, you will be my witness to this,
when a woman dies to match my woman's death,
when a man falls to match that other man,
whose wife was his assassin.
This friendly office I lay on you, as I die now.   1320

Chorus

Poor girl, I pity you for your death,
that the god predicted.

Cassandra

I have one more speech to make,
or shall I call it a dirge, just for myself.
As I face this last sunlight,
I call on those who shall be my avengers
to make my enemies pay for *my* murder too,
only a dead slave, such an easy victory.
Men's fortunes, when they are good,
one might say of them, "They are like shadows only."
When they're bad, a wet sponge
with one stroke wipes it all out.
The first truth has my pity, far more than the second.   1330

(*Exit Cassandra.*)

Chorus

To be successful is to be endlessly hungry for more;
all men are so.

There is no one who banishes good fortune from his house,
so long as fingers point at it.
No man says, "Do not come here again, good fortune."
Here is this king, to whom the blessed gods granted
the sacking of Priam's city;
he came home with all the honors that the gods gave him.
But now, if he shall pay for the blood of the past
and dying render the price of others' deaths,
who that hears this and must die himself
dare boast that a man may be born
to live a whole life unharmed?

Agamemnon (*from within*)

I've been hit! I am hurt to death. 1340

Chorus

Hush! Who is it that cries out, hurt to death?

Agamemnon

I'm hit again!

Chorus

It is the king crying out; I think all is over.
But let us plan safety for ourselves—if we can.
1. My vote is to cry, Help! to the citizens
to come to the palace.
2. Yes, and at once, I think, 1350
to catch them red-handed with dripping sword.
3. I think you're right; at least we should do something.
It certainly isn't the moment for hesitation.
4. But we can see. This is a kind of first act;
it looks like the beginning of a tyranny.
5. Yes, it does—because we're wasting time.
Their hands don't sleep, and they trample underfoot
the good reputation of delay.
6. I really do not know what would be best.
Those who do the deed of course find it easy to plan.
7. Yes, I am with you. Anyhow, 1360
one cannot by talking bring the dead to life again.

8. Are we then, in order to stretch our own lives,
to yield to a government that shames our royal house?
9. No, that is awful. Death is better than that.
Death is better than subjection to a tyranny.
10. Is the evidence of the cries good enough?
Are we right to predict that the man is dead?
11. Yes, one must know before one gets angry.
Knowing the truth is very far from guessing.
12. I have the support of many voices among you: 1370
that we should be told clearly how it is with Agamemnon.

(Enter Clytemnestra.)

Clytemnestra
　　Till now I have said much to meet the occasion,
but now I will not be ashamed to say the opposite.
How could one, rendering hate to those who hated
but looked like loved ones,
hedge the trap about with sides too high to be leapt over?
This was my day of trial; I have thought of it
enough and long enough, a trial of an old quarrel
years and years old.
Now I stand here where I have struck him.
He is dead, and the sequence ended.
This is how I managed—I will not disavow it—   1380
that he should not escape, nor defend himself from death.
I threw about him an encompassing net,
as it might be for fish, all-entangling,
an evil wealth of cloak.
I struck him twice. He gave two groans,
and his body went limp;
as he lay there, I gave him a third,
in honor of the Zeus that keeps the dead
securely in the underworld.
This was my grace and prayer for him.
So, as he lay there, he gasped out his spirit,   1390
choking, poured out a sharp stream of his blood
and struck me with the dark bloody shower.

I rejoiced as much as the new-sown earth
rejoices in the glad rain of Zeus,
when the buds strike in earth's womb.
So it is, you old men of Argos here;
be glad, if you can. I triumph in it.
If it were right to pour libations
on a dead man's body, I would have done so to him,
and more than justly done so.
Here's a bowl of horrors, cursed horrors,
that he filled within our house,
and then he came and drank it off himself.

Chorus

   I wonder at your tongue, how boldly it wags,
   that you should boast like this over a dead husband.

Clytemnestra

   You try me out as if I were   1400
   a woman that cannot think.
   But my heart doesn't tremble,
   and I speak to you who know;
   whether you wish to praise or blame me is all one to me.
   Here is Agamemnon, my husband, now a corpse—
   his death the work of this right hand of mine,
   an efficient craftsman.
   That is how *that* is.

Chorus

   Woman, what evil thing have you eaten
   that grows in the earth,
   what draught have you tasted that comes from the salt sea,
   that you have taken upon you so horrible a sacrifice
   and the curse of the people's voice?
   You have cast away, you have torn apart,   1410
   and you shall be cast and torn away from the city,
   a monstrous object of hate to the citizens.

Clytemnestra

   Now it's against me that you proclaim banishment,
   that the hatred and curses of the citizens shall be mine,

but in the old days you brought nothing against that man,
who, with all the indifference of one whose pastures are full
of teeming flocks, rich in wool,
had no care for the death of a lamb.
He sacrificed his own daughter,
dearest pain of my womb,
to charm the contrariness of Thracian winds.
For this, should you not have banished him,
payment for his polluting wickedness?
No, you are a careful hearer and harsh judge   1420
only of *my* acts.
Threaten away! I tell you now, if once you conquer me
in a fair fight, I'll be your subject;
but if God gives another outcome,
you will get an education in discretion
and learn it thoroughly, though the knowledge
comes very late.

Chorus

You think big thoughts, and you scream proud defiance,
as though the bloody smear of your success
had maddened your mind.
The smear of blood—I can see it in your eyes.
But still you must pay stroke for stroke,
with no friend to take your part.

Clytemnestra

You may now hear the solemn swearing of my oath: 1430
By the justice due to my child, and now perfected,
by the Spirit of Destruction and the Fury,
in whose honor I cut this man's throat,
my hope treads not within the hall of Fear
so long as Aegisthus lights the hearth fire for me,
my loyal friend, as he has always been,
shield for my daring—no small one.
There lies Agamemnon, this girl's seducer—
he was the darling of all the women of Troy—
and there she is, our prophet, prisoner of war,   1440

that shared his bed, a faithful whore
that spoke her auguries for him, and knew as well
the rubbing of the sailors' benches.
Both have suffered as they deserved.
He died as I said, and she has sung her swan song in death,
and lies with him, her lover.
But to me she has brought an additional side dish
to *my* pleasure in bed.

Chorus

What day of doom may I look for soon,
one with not too much pain, not too long bedridden,
that shall bring me the sleep that has no ending,
now that my kindest of guardians has been overcome,   1450
suffering so much at a woman's hands.
By a woman his life has perished.
Curse on you, crazy Helen, that were the single murderess
of all those lives, those many lives,
lost under Troy's walls;
now you have made the fulfillment,
the fine flowering, of whatever it was,
that quarrel within the house
built to bring a man to misery.
You have perfected it,   1460
through bloodshed that cannot be washed out.

Clytemnestra

Do not pray for your end in death
because of the burden of your grief in this,
nor turn your anger against Helen,
as the man-killer who destroyed
those many lives of the Greeks,
and brought into being an incurable pain.

Chorus

Spirit that attacks the house of the sons of Atreus,
you master me to the breaking of my heart;
your power is wielded by two women of like soul.   1470

85

And now you stand like an evil raven,
and croak over the dead a lawless hymn of victory.

Clytemnestra

Now indeed you have made right
the judgment of your mouth,
as you name the thrice-glutted spirit of this race.
It is through him that the love of blood-licking
is nourished in the belly,
and before the old wound has healed,
new pus comes.

Chorus

Yes, the one you name is indeed great,   1480
the spirit whose anger lies heavy on this house.
And the tale you have to tell is evil;
it has an endless appetite for the events of blind madness.
But surely these are through Zeus,
who is cause of all, who brings all to pass.
For what is there that is fulfilled for man,
except through Zeus?
What is there of all this
that is not of God's accomplishment?
O my king, my king,   1490
how shall I sorrow for you?
What shall I say from a heart that loves you?
You lie there in that spider's web,
gasping out your life in an unholy death.
Oh, oh! Conquered by deadly treachery,
to fall to such an ignoble bed
by a wife's hand and a double-edged blade.

Clytemnestra

You cry aloud on this as *my* work;
but do not call me Agamemnon's wife.
No, it is the old, bitter, Evil Genius   1500
of Atreus, giver of the cruel feast,
that has likened himself to the wife of this dead man

and has paid him off, sacrificing a full-grown victim
in fulfillment for those young children.

Chorus

But who will bear you witness
that you are guiltless of the murder?
How, how so? It is true, there may be,
on his father's side, the Evil Genius to help you.
And the black god of war presses on
through tides of kindred blood
to the place of his advance,
where he pays just requital
for the congealed fragments of the eaten children.
O my king, my king,   1510
how shall I sorrow for you?
What shall I say from a heart that loves you?
You lie there in that spider's web,
gasping out your life in an unholy death.
Oh, oh! Conquered by deadly treachery,
to fall to such an ignoble bed
by a wife's hand and a double-edged blade.

Clytemnestra

Did *he* not also lay upon the house   1520
a treacherous destruction?
The victim, my daughter, raised from his loins,
Iphigeneia, whom I mourn for.
What he did is what he suffered for.
Let him not boast of anything in the house of death,
for he paid for what he had done
with death by the mischief of the sword.

Chorus

I am all bewildered about what road to take   1530
as the house falls;
my wits are deserted by their skillful carefulness.
I fear the crash of the bloody torrent of rain
that will shake the house to its foundation.
Now it is a shower no longer.

Fate is whetting its justice on other whetstones
for another deed of injury.
Earth, Earth, would you had received me   1540
before I lived to see him in his lowly couch
in a silver-sided bath.
Who shall bury him? Who shall keen him?
Will you dare to do this, to make lament for him,
you who killed him, your husband?
Will you accomplish for his soul a grace no grace
as thanks for his great deeds?
Who shall stand at the grave and chant
a praise of the hero
with tears in the eye and truthful sorrow at heart?

Clytemnestra

The care of that concerns you not at all.   1550
It is by our hand that he fell, that he died,
and we shall bury him
with no cries of mourning from this house.
But his daughter Iphigeneia, as is right,
will welcome her father by the swift-flowing passage
over the River of Sorrows
and throw her arms around him and kiss him.

Chorus

This is but the exchange of insult for insult;   1560
it is hard to judge the issue of such a fight.
The pirate plunders the pirate,
the killer pays for the killing.
Still there remains, as long as Zeus remains on his throne,
the rule that he who has acted shall suffer accordingly.
That is the divine law.
Who shall expel from the house the brood of curses?
The whole race is welded to destruction.

Clytemnestra

In what you say now, the prophecy has become truth.
For my part, I am willing to make a sworn compact   1570
with the evil spirit of this house

to be satisfied with things as they are, however bad,
on condition that he, in the days to come,
may go from our house and wear out some other breed
with murders of one another in the family.
I will be utterly content with a small part of wealth,
if I can banish from these halls
the madness of mutual bloodletting.

(*Enter Aegisthus.*)

Aegisthus

O happy light, day of justified revenge!
Now I will say that the gods
in watchfulness so high above the earth
still bear an eye on the sorrows of mortals to avenge them.
Now I take pleasure to have seen this man   1580
lying here in the robes that were
the nets of the Furies for him,
paying for the plots his father's hand contrived.
For Atreus, ruler of this land, was this man's father,
and his brother Thyestes was my father.
Both were Pelops's sons; this is the plain story.
The two of them were in dispute about the throne,
and Atreus banished my father from city and home.
The unlucky Thyestes later returned,
a suppliant at Atreus's hearth, and found safety there—
I mean for his own part, for he did not die
nor stained his fatherland with blood.
But the vile Atreus, father of the dead man here,   1590
with show of eagerness rather than love,
gave my father a banquet of welcome.
He pretended to celebrate a day of feasting
on flesh slaughtered for meat,
in all hospitality,
but the meat he gave my father was his own children's.
The feet and the ends of the fingers he put apart and hid,
as the guests sat man by man at separate tables.
So Thyestes in ignorance ate the other parts,

a meal that brought a curse, as you see, on all the race.
Later, when he discovered what awful act he had committed,
he moaned aloud, recoiled, and vomited up the bloody mess.
"A doom intolerable will overtake," he said,   1600
"the house of Pelops."
He kicked the dinner over to back the oath,
crying, "So perish every one of all your breed."
That is why you can see this man fallen dead here,
and I am justly the one who stitched together his murder.
I was the third son, and while I was still in swaddling clothes
he drove me out along with my luckless father.
But when I grew to manhood, justice brought me back.
And so I laid my hand on him, though not face to face;
mine was the whole contriving of the evil plot.
So glorious the result,   1610
that now I would welcome death itself,
having seen him in the traps of justice.

Chorus

Aegisthus, I do not respect insolence
at the moment of calamity.
Do you say that with aforethought you killed Agamemnon,
that you alone planned this miserable murder?
In that case, I do not think your life will escape
the justice of the public curse, the stoning.
 That's what I think.

Aegisthus

Do you talk back to me, you who sit at the lower oar,
when we are in possession of the upper deck?
You will find out, despite your age,
how uncomfortable such learning is for an old man,
when discretion is the lesson set.
Chains in old age and hunger's pangs   1620
are the very sharpest healing prophets of the mind.
Don't you see this when you see?
Kick not against the pricks, lest your own striking hurts you.

Chorus
    Woman, you who were his housekeeper
    and at the same time sullied his bed,
      did you plot his death when the victors were newly home
    and he had been their general?
Aegisthus
    These words of yours are true progenitors of sorrows.   1630
    Yours is a tongue the opposite of Orpheus's:
    he led all things his captive through the joy of his own voice,
    but you with silly yappings arouse others to lead *you* captive.
    Once you are mastered, you'll be a tamer animal.
Chorus
    I suppose you'll be the sovereign of the Argives,
    you, who when you plotted this man's murder
    didn't dare to do the deed with your own hand.
Aegisthus
    Well, no. The treachery was a woman's part,
    clearly so. I would be suspected as his old enemy.
    But his wealth will give me a base to rule the citizens,   1640
    and the disobedient man I will yoke in heavy chains;
    he will not be, I assure you, like a full-fed young trace horse.
    No, unwelcome hunger and a dark cell
    will see him through into submission.
Chorus
    Why didn't you kill him yourself, with your cowardly soul?
    No, your partner, the woman, did the killing,
    to be the pollution of the land and of the gods of the land.
    But I tell you, Orestes still sees the light of day,
    that he may come home, and with good luck on his side
    be conquerer and the death of both of you.
Aegisthus
    Since you're resolved to act and talk like this,
    you'll soon know—
    here, my bodyguards, this is your work, right here.

Chorus

 Here, let each one of you be ready, hand on   1650
 sword hilt.

Aegisthus

 I, too, hold the hilt of my sword.
 I will face my death.

Chorus

 You talk of death; I welcome it. But I will try my chances.

Clytemnestra

 No, dearest, no. Let us do no further evils.
 Those that there are, are many, a bloody harvest;
 we have a good store of calamity.
 No, no bloodletting.
 Good old men, off with you to your houses.
 Yield to what must be, before you suffer.
 What we did had to be done.
 If this should be all of troubles, I would gladly welcome it,
 though struck with misfortune
 by the heavy hoof of the evil spirit.
 That is a woman's word, if anyone should think it
 worth heeding.

Aegisthus

 No, but to have them letting their tongues   1660
 blossom in insolence, to throw their empty threats about—
 "That they would try their chances"—
 You lack all brains, so to abuse your master.

Chorus

 It does not fit an Argive to fawn on a villian.

Aegisthus

 I will get even with you in the days to come.

Chorus

 Not if the Spirit brings Orestes home.

Aegisthus

 I know the diet of exiles is rich in hope.

Chorus

 Yes, do things, grow fat, pollute justice—while you can.

Aegisthus
You know you will pay me for your foolishness.　　　　1670
Chorus
Boast, do; be bold—a cock beside your hen.
Clytemnestra
Do not pay heed to their vain yappings. I
and you together will make all things well,
for we are masters of this house.

THE LIBATION BEARERS
DRAMATIS PERSONAE

Orestes,
son of King Agamemnon

Pylades,
friend of Orestes

Electra,
daughter of King Agamemnon

Chorus,
captives of war in Argos,
friends of Electra

Servant of the house

Nurse of Orestes

Clytemnestra

Aegisthus

THE LIBATION BEARERS

(Enter Orestes and Pylades.)

Orestes
> Hermes, god of the underworld,
> Hermes, protector of my father's sovereign rights,
> be now my savior, my ally, as I supplicate you.
> For I come to this land a returned exile,
> and here upon this mound, my father's grave,
> I call on him to give ear to me and hear.
> I dedicated a lock of my hair to Inachus for nurture,
> and here is another, this time for mourning.
> For, father, I wasn't there to raise my voice
> in sorrow at your death.
> I did not stretch out my hand
> in the funeral greeting.

(Enter Electra and Chorus.)

> What is this I see?   10
> What is this band of women
> all in black, marching by so conspicuously?
> What can have happened? What does it look like?
> What new disaster can have struck the house?
> They seem to be bringing soothing libations for the dead;
> that must be it.
> For I see my sister Electra coming,
> in deep mourning as she would be.
> O Zeus, grant that I may avenge my father!
> Be my ally, in all graciousness.
> Pylades, let us stand aside here,   20
> so we may find out truly what this is,
> this procession of women.

(They stand aside.)

Chorus
> From the house I was sent to lead the procession
> which brings the libations.

You can see our sharp fingernails are weary
from plowing new furrows on our cheeks
till they're torn and bloody.
Always the heart finds its meat in endless lamentation.
The robes at our breasts torn to linen shreds,
the sound of the tearing rags speaks our grief.
But we are stricken with sorrow for what happens,   30
and our faces laugh no more.
Sharp and hair-raising the cry of a prophetic dream,
raising from sleep at dead of night, breathing anger,
it screams terror from the depths of the house;
it falls heavily on the women's quarters.
The dream-interpreters trusted to speak for the gods   40
scream, "The dead beneath the earth blame us;
they are angry against their killers."
O Mother Earth, here is a graceless grace to avert evil,
sought by this godless woman who has sent us.
I fear to utter this word.
For how can one expiate blood fallen on the earth?
O hearth in utter misery,
O house dug down in ruin,
sunless darkness that hates mankind   50
envelops the house in the deaths of its lords.
In the old days there was reverence,
something stronger than fighting, war, or conquest.
It penetrated the ears and minds of the people.
It is gone now. There is fear—yes.
There is success, and that among men   60
is a god, and more than a god.
But there is a balance-scale of justice that keeps watch,
quickly on some in the light of day,
and pain waits for others between light and darkness,
and still others are held by the night of unfulfillment.
For blood that the earth has drunk into itself,
a murder of requital has been fixed and will not dissolve.
It continues to haunt the guilty man with ruin,

in a disease always luxuriant.
For him also that pollutes the bed of bridal love,   70
there is no remedy;
all tracks lead to the one road,
and in vain would they cleanse
the hand that is infected.
On me the god has brought the constraint
of belonging to two cities—from my father's house
to this slavery; and in just things and unjust
I must submit to authority fiercely carried.
I will control the bitterness of my heart.
But beneath my cloak I weep   80
at the lechery of my masters,
and I am chilled with secret sorrow.

Electra

Ladies in waiting that tend my house,
since you are here as part of the procession,
give me your counsel in this matter.
What am I to say as I pour the libation of mourning?
How can I speak with good will, how pray to my father?
Can I say, coming from *my* mother,   90
"A gift from a loving wife to loving husband"?
I haven't the audacity for that.
I cannot tell what I should say,
as I pour the oils on my father's grave.
Shall it be the usual prayer of mankind?—
"Grant to those that sent the garlands an antidote
to match the evils that occasioned the gifts."
Or shall I, in dishonoring silence
—as indeed my father died—
throw the liquid for earth to drink
and go away like someone throwing out dirt,
and with it hurl the vessel, with averted eyes?
My friends, be my partners in counsel.   100
For ours is a common grief for the house;
do not through fear of anyone

hide your thoughts in your heart.
For fate awaits alike the free
and the one who lives under a master's hand.
Speak, if you've anything better to say
than I have said.

Chorus

I will speak then, since you bid me,
for this grave of your father I revere like an altar,
and my words will be what's in my mind.

Electra

Speak, just as you revere my father's grave.

Chorus

Pour the holy oils, and say:
"To those that are his well-wishers—"

Electra

Whom shall I address as that,   110
amongst his friends?

Chorus

First yourself, and then whoever hates Aegisthus.

Electra

So my prayer will be for me and for you?

Chorus

You know this yourself; speak it immediately.

Electra

Whom shall I add besides, to our faction?

Chorus

Remember Orestes, even if he is not here.

Electra

Good, good! How well you do instruct me.

Chorus

Then remember—"On those guilty of the murder—"

Electra

What shall I say?- I don't know. Tell me.

Chorus

Pray that on them there come a god or a man—

Electra

    As judge or as avenger? Which shall I say?   120

Chorus

    Say simply, "Who will kill to answer killing?"

Electra

    Can I with piety ask the gods for that?

Chorus

    Yes, giving evil for evil to an enemy.

Electra

    Greatest herald of all above or below the earth,

    Hermes of the underworld,

    summon the spirits under earth, who keep their watch

    over my father's house, to hear my prayer.

    And Earth herself, that brings all things to birth,

    and having raised them takes again from them

    the fruit of their fertility—

    here I, that pour to the dead this oil,

    call to my father: Father, have pity on me.

    Kindle dear Orestes to be a light to the house.   130

    For as it is, both of us are exiles,

    sold by our mother, who has traded us for her man,

    Aegisthus, her partner in our father's murder.

    Myself, I might as well be a slave.

    Orestes is banished from his property,

    while they grow rich and insolent amidst our troubles.

    I pray you that Orestes may come here

    with luck to back him.

    O my father, hear me.

    Grant that I may be more chaste than my mother,   140

    and have a hand more reverent than hers.

    So far, my prayers for us; but upon our enemies

    I pray, my father, that you come avenging

    and bring a death with justice on the killers.

    I set this prayer for evil, speaking against my enemies,

    in the midst of the prayer for good.

But Hermes be the bringer of good to us in the upper world,
with the help of the gods and earth and conquering justice.
(She pours out the libations.)
These are my prayers, and there the libation poured.
(Speaking to the Chorus.)
It is the custom that you sing the hymn   150
to crown the mourning in honor of the dead.
Chorus

Drop the streaming tear for a death,
for dead is our lord;
drop the tear that shall be a shield for us
to help the good avert the ill,
the curse of terror;
for now the offerings are poured.
Hear me, lord whom I revere,
hear me in the infirmity of my mind.
Let one come to redeem the house,
a man strong with the spear;
let him brandish in his hand a Scythian bow;   160
let him wield as well
the sword for fighting hand to hand.
Electra

My father has the oils;
the earth has drunk them.

(She sees the lock of Orestes' hair.)
But here is new matter for a story;
share this, also with me.
Chorus

Speak. My heart is dancing with fear.
Electra

I see on the grave a lock of newly cut hair.
Chorus

From what man's head, or what deep-breasted girl's?
Electra

That is a riddle anyone could guess.   170

Chorus
Not I; tell me. I am old and you are young.
Electra
No one but myself could have cut off this hair.
Chorus
True, those who should mourn him so
are all his enemies.
Electra
Yet certainly it looks very like—
Chorus
Like whose hair? Tell me what you see in it.
Electra
Certainly it much *resembles* mine.
Chorus
Could it be a secret gift from him, Orestes?
Electra
It is very, very like his hair.
Chorus
How could he have dared to come here?
Electra
He *sent* it—this hair,   180
a mourning tribute to his father.
Chorus
We have as much occasion to cry as ever,
if his foot shall never touch this land again.
Electra
A wave of bitter gall has settled on my heart;
it is as if a sword had pierced me through.
The thirsty drops fall from my eyes—
they cannot be held back, flood tide of winter water—
as I look at this hair.
How can I believe that someone else among the people here
owns hair like this? Surely, she that killed him
would hardly cut her hair to mourn him—
my mother, whose godless spirit disowns   190

the name of mother for her children.
But how can I say without a doubt
that this precious thing must belong to Orestes—
dearest to me in all the world?
Surely, hope begins to flatter me.
Oh, if only the hair could take a human voice
and play the messenger,
that I might not, as now, be in two minds and waver;
then either it would bid me clearly
cast out this hair in loathing,
if it were truly a cutting from an enemy's head,
or, being kindred, it could mourn with me,
a decoration to this grave and honor to my father.
We call on gods that know   200
in what storms, like sailors,
we are tossed and twisted. If we are to be saved,
a small seed may grow into a mightly trunk.
Look, look! Here is some more evidence—
footprints, and they are also like mine.
Here are two pairs of tracks
outlined—his, and some other traveler's with him.
The imprint of the heels and the arches
measures exactly with mine
when I place my foot in the prints.
This is agony and craziness.

                                        (*Orestes enters.*)   210
Orestes
   Pray for the rest, that it may turn out well,
   acknowledging the prayers that are fulfilled.
Electra
   As of now, what have I got with the help of the gods?
Orestes
   You have come in sight of
   what you long have prayed for.
Electra
   Do you know whom I have called upon?

Orestes
  I know that you dearly love Orestes.
Electra
  And how does that mean my prayers are answered?
Orestes
  I am he. Do not look for any man   220
  more loved than me.
Electra
  Is this some trick, sir, that you are playing upon me?
Orestes
  If so, it is a trick upon myself.
Electra
  You want to make a mockery of my sorrows.
Orestes
  If I mock your sorrows, I would mock my own.
Electra
  Can I be talking to you, the real Orestes?
Orestes
  You see me in person, and don't know me.
  But you saw the mourning lock of hair,
  you trod in my footprints, tracking me out,
  and then you were ecstatic, you were sure you saw me.
  Look here, put the lock of cut hair next to your own;
  and *this (indicating a lock of his hair)* is a match,
  your brother's hair.
  Look at this piece of woven cloth, your handiwork,   230
  your shuttle struck it on the loom;
  the beasts are your embroidered pictures.
  Control yourself. Do not let joy
  quite overcome your wits.
  For those who should be dearest
  hate us both.
Electra
  O dearest darling of your father's house,
  the tearful hope of the saving seed,
  trust in your strength and you will still

win back that house.
O delightful face that has
all four shares of my love:
I must call you father, and to you belongs   240
the love due to a mother, too—
I hate her, quite justly—
and to you belongs, as well,
the love for my sister, ruthlessly sacrificed;
and you are my brother, trusted and honored
as no one else. May Victory, Justice,
and Zeus, making the third, greatest of all,
be your helpers; so I would have it.

Orestes

Zeus, Zeus, look down and save us!
Behold the brood who have lost their eagle father,
killed in the folds and coils of the deadly viper.
We are orphaned nestlings, and the hunger pinches;   250
we are not yet fit to bring home what our fathers hunted.
So I and you, dear Electra, can be seen here—
a family without a father—
both sharers of the same exile at home.
Yet, Zeus, my father was your worshiper,
honored you greatly with his sacrifices,
and if you now destroy his children,
where will you find a hand so generous to give feasts?
If you blot out the eagle's breed, you will nevermore
have signs to send to mortals such as will win belief.
Nor will this trunk, this princely stock,   260
if wholly withered, serve your altars
on days of sacrifice of cattle.
Save us! You will lift this house to greatness
that now is small, indeed would seem quite fallen.

Chorus

Children, saviors of your father's hearth,
silence, lest someone hear you, children,
and through delight in talking bring the news

to the masters of the house—Oh, to see *them*
dead in a fiery ooze of pitch!
Orestes
    The strong oracle of Apollo will not let me down,   270
that oracle that bade me run this risk.
He spoke of many things in his warning voice,
of chill destruction under the warm heart,
if I should fail to pursue my father's murderers
in their own fashion;
"Kill them," he said, "to match their killings,
you who are driven to madness
by the loss of your inheritance."
Otherwise, he said, with my own life
I myself would pay, with a multitude of dreadful sufferings.
Some of what he told me was of the anger of evil spirits
from under the earth, malignant against mortals,
diseases on us both, that would climb on our flesh
with savage jaws, cankers that eat into our bodies' nature,
and a white down on top of the sick parts.
Of all assaults of the Furies he spoke,   280
that my father's blood would bring to bear upon me
as I gaze clearly into the darkness, with eyebrows active.
For the arrow of those below, that flies in darkness,
winged by the prayers of the kindred of those dead,
and madness, and empty terrors waking at night,
drive with the bronze-plated scourge, haunt,
and chase from the city the tortured body.
Such people have no share nor partnership   290
in the libation bowl, nor the rich wine poured out.
The unseen anger of the father bars his son from the altars;
none may welcome him nor lodge with him.
And at the last, unhonored and unloved,
in utter ruin, wasted to dryness, death.
Should I not believe the truth of oracles like these?
Even if I didn't belive, the deed must be done.
For there are many desires converging in one,   300

the gods' commands, my great grief for my father—
and I am pinched by loss of my property—
the thought that those most famous of mankind,
the citizens who devastated Troy in spirit of glory,
shall become subjects of two women.
His (i.e., Aegisthus's) spirit is womanish. If it is not,
he will soon know what he is.

Chorus

O great fates, bring all to fulfillment
through Zeus in the way that the path of justice is.
Let enemy tongue pay for enemy tongue;
justice in exaction of a debt has a loud voice.
For bloody stroke, let a bloody stroke be paid.   310
"He who acts shall suffer"—
this is the voice of the story grown old in time.

Orestes

Father, father most dread,
what shall I say or do
to bring you here from your far land
where the bed of the grave holds you,
where darkness is your share of the light,
where the eulogy of the mourners
is called joy and comfort
for the sons of Atreus, former princes of this house?

Chorus

Child, the fierce, devouring jaw of fire   320
does not devour the spirit of the dead man;
no, he shows his anger later.
The dying man is mourned,
he that did the injury is discovered;
the due mourning of fathers and parents,
poured in abundance overflowing,
shall set the hunt on.

Electra

Hear, O my father, in turn,   330
my grief and my tears.

Hear the twin dirge of your children by the graveside.
The grave has welcomed us,
as suppliant and exile, both alike.
What of this is well? What is without evil?
What is not our destruction,
our third fall in wrestling?

Chorus

Yet still from all this, if the god so wills,   340
he may bring to pass more tuneful songs,
and instead of dirges at the grave
a hymn of welcome shall greet
the loving cup in the royal palace.

Orestes

Would that under Troy's walls, father,
you had been cut down by the spear of some Lycian soldier.
Then you would have left in your house
a fair fame, and established for your children
in their goings to and fro
a life for all to admire.
And you yourself would have had   350
a mounded grave in the land overseas
that your house could support with honor.

Chorus

Then would you be loved of those whom you loved
who are in the house of death, who have died gloriously;
beneath the earth, you would be a prince of dreadful honor,
presiding among the greatest
of those kings of the underworld;
for you were a king in life,   360
even one of those whose hands were filled
with the giving of the doom of death
and the scepter that wins men's allegiance.

Electra

Yes, father, would that beneath Troy's walls
you had died with the rest of the spear-slaughtered host,
and found your burial by the ford of Scamander.

But I had rather those who killed you
should have died as you died,
and some of us from afar off heard of it
as a tale of things that never touched us.
Chorus
  In that, my child, you speak of something   370
  greater than gold, a great chance
  and a greater bliss.
  Certainly you can *speak* of it,
  but there comes the sound of the stroke
  of the double lash.
  The champions of the one side are even now under the earth,
  and the hands of the masters of the house are unholy—
  those hateful creatures—
  and grow more so against the children.
Orestes
  This has struck me to the heart like an arrow.   380
  Zeus, O Zeus, send up to us from the world below
  revenge, even though it be late in coming,
  on the violent sacrilegious hand—
  revenge to be perfected again on the parents.
Chorus
  May it be mine to sing a strong cry of triumph
  over a man stricken and a woman dying.
  Why should I hide the hope which flutters in my breast
  despite me?
  Sharp blows the rage before the portals of my heart—   390
  long-cherished hatred.
Electra
  When will the hand of Zeus strike with power?
  When will he split the head?
  Let it come in such form as the land can believe.
  After the days of injustice I demand justice.
  Hear me, Earth, and you dignitaries of the underworld.
Chorus
  It is the law that the drops of blood   400

fallen on the ground demand more blood.
The plague of the Furies calls aloud
on behalf of those already dead
for another destruction to crown the first.

Orestes

Alas, Earth, sovereignties of the underworld,
you all-mastering curses of the dead,
look upon us, look upon the remnants
of the stock of Atreus, so perplexed.
Look upon the dishonor of the house.
Whom shall one turn to, O Zeus?

Chorus

My loving heart is shaken again   410
when I hear this pitiable cry;
my hope fails me; my heart grows blacker
as I listen. But when I see you
armed for action,
lightly my hope has torn away sorrow
as I greet the appearance of good fortune.

Electra

What shall we say and win our prayer?
Shall it be all we have suffered from our mother?
We can flatter, but the others are not charmed.   420
I have a spirit like a ravening wolf's;
I got it from my savage-minded mother.

Chorus

Like a woman of the East, and with Oriental dirges,
I beat my breast, mourning.
The strokes of my hand come thick and fast;
one can see the traces of the gripping, tearing nails,
up and down, up and down, and my wretched head rings
in answering the sound of the blows.

Electra

O mother, all-daring, you were his enemy,   430
and you dared to give him an enemy's funeral;

without citizens for the carrying forth of their king,
without dirge you buried him, unmourned.

Orestes

Indeed, utterly without honor is
the burying you tell of;
but she shall pay for the dishonoring of my father,
by favor of the gods, by favor of these hands of mine.
When I have cut my foes away from life,
may my death come upon me.

Chorus

She cut off his hands to stuff in his armpits,   440
let me tell you; she did that,
she who buried him as you say,
seeking to render his death something
unbearable to you, his children.
What I tell you is your father's dishonored agony.

Electra

You speak of my father's death; but I stood apart,
dishonored, worthless. I was shut up
in a corner of the house, like a vicious dog.
I found a stream of tears readier than laughter;
I poured out my tears in flood in secret.
Hear this, my father, and write it
in the tablets of your mind.

Chorus

Drive the word through the ears   450
to the steadying pace of the mind.
These things are surely so;
but more one would wish to learn.
We must proceed with unbending spirit.

Orestes

I bid you, father, come to us—
we love you.

Electra

I have given you my tears;
I invite you.

Chorus

> And we chime in, a band of friends
> that joins with them.
> Hear us and come to the light,
> come to us against your enemies.

Orestes

> War god will clash with war god,   460
> Justice with Justice.

Electra

> O gods, grant just fulfillment!

Chorus

> I begin to tremble as I hear these prayers.
> The fated moment has waited so long,
> but it may come in answer to their prayers.
> O evil, bred in the stock,
> harsh bloody stroke of destruction,
> mournful agony unbearable,
> pain that cannot be put to rest!
> The cure for these sorrows is in the house;   470
> it must come from them, not from outside;
> it must come from savage bloody strife itself.
> This is the hymn of the Powers beneath the earth.
> Hear me, you Blessed Ones of the Underworld;
> give helpful escort to these children's prayers
> and lead them graciously to victory.

Orestes

> Father, killed in ways unroyal,
> give me control of the house that was yours!

Electra

> I, too, Father, need this from you—   480
> to destroy Aegisthus and to escape.

Orestes

> If this should be, then will your feasts
> be kept among mankind in all due order.
> But if it should not be so, then will you be

without honor among the well-feasted gods
on earth, without a share in the fat sacrifices.

Electra

I, too, will bring you out of my dowry
libations from my father's house,
at my marriage.
This grave will have the primacy of honor.

Orestes

O Earth, send up my father to oversee the fight!

Electra

Persephone, grant us a graceful victory!   490

Orestes

Remember the bath in which you died, my father.

Electra

Remember the robes, put to new use as a net.

Orestes

Chains not of bronze held you, my father,
hunted to death.

Electra

Caught you shamefully in treacherous robes,
as in a trap.

Orestes

Will these taunts rouse you from your sleep, my father?

Electra

Will you lift up your beloved head?

Orestes

Send us Justice, as an ally to those who love you!
Grant us a handhold to match *their* hands
if you, now conquered, want your
turn for victory!

Electra

Hear this last cry of all, my father: 500
Look on the nestlings, here upon your grave.
Have pity on your brood, both male and female.

Orestes

Do not blot out this seed of Pelops's children.

For if they live you are not dead, in death.
Children are voices of salvation to a dead man;
they are like corks that keep the nets afloat,
saving the woven meshes from the depths.

Electra
Hear—it is for you we raise our sorrowful song.
You will save yourself if you listen to our prayers.

Chorus
Truly, this honor to the unsorrowed grave   510
has lasted long enough,
though none can fault you two for that.
But now, since you are rightly set on action,
you should try your fortune at once, and act.

Orestes
We will, but it is not amiss to know
why she has sent the offerings, what story moved her
to pay for an inexpiable crime
so many years after. Surely, a wretched favor
is this, sent to the insensitive dead man.
I cannot guess the meaning of these offerings,
but they are surely less than the offense.
If one were to spill everything in the world   520
to cure the bloodletting of one man,
the labor is lost, men say. But tell me what I ask,
if so be that you know it.

Chorus
Yes, I know it,
my son, for I was there. That godless woman
was driven by dreams and by night-wandering terrors
to send these offerings.

Orestes
Did you find out about her dream,
to be able to tell it rightly?

Chorus
She thought that she gave birth to a snake—
that is how she told it.

Orestes
How did her story end? How did it come out?
Chorus
She wrapped the snake in swaddling clothes,
like a baby.
Orestes
What food did it need, this newborn monster?   530
Chorus
She gave it the breast, in her dream.
Orestes
How did the hateful thing not hurt the nipple?
Chorus
It did. It drew clots of blood with the milk.
Orestes
This is not meaningless! It is a vision of a man.
Chorus
She started out of her sleep and cried in terror,
and many a lamp that was blinded in darkness
blazed in the palace walls to pleasure its mistress.
And after that, she sent these funeral offerings;
she hoped that they would cure all that was wrong.
Orestes
This is *my* prayer, by this land,   540
by my father's grave:
may this dream find fulfillment for me!
I judge it will, too; all of it fits.
For if the snake came from the same place *I* did,
and wore my swaddling clothes, and sucked the breast
that gave me sustenance, mixed the dear milk
with clots of blood, and she was terrified
at what had happened—then, it must be so that,
as she raised this fearful monster,
she must die violently!
For I that became that very snake will kill her,
even as the dream has said.

Chorus
I'll take your reading of these signs,   550
and so may it turn out! For the rest,
instruct us that are your friends—
tell some what to do, and others what not to do.
Orestes
It is a simply story. My sister must go inside—
I tell her, hide this plan we have arranged—
that those who killed with treachery a prince
may themselves be caught with treachery and die
in the same snare—as Loxias has prophesied,
our Lord, Apollo, that from old times never lied.
I will disguise myself as a foreigner,   560
with all the traveler's gear,
and come with Pylades here to the courtyard gates.
I will be a guest-friend and ally of the house.
We will both speak with a Parnassian accent.
Even if none of the sentries will be eager to receive us,
as the house is so bedeviled with trouble
—yet we will stand and wait, until
some passerby will guess at who we are
and say, "Why does Aegisthus bar his door
against a suppliant—if he is really at home
and knows of it?"
And if once I cross the threshold   570
of the courtyard gates, if once I find him
upon my father's throne, or if he comes to speak
to me, face to face, or calls me to his presence,
before he says, "Where is this foreigner from?"
with my quick blade I will send him to his death.
The Fury unstinted of murder will now drink
a third draught of blood full strength, undiluted.
Do you, Electra, keep careful watch in the house,
so that our plans will fit with one another.
You, my friends, keep   580

a very heedful hold upon your tongue.
There is a season for silence and for necessary speech.
The rest Pylades here must oversee,
who has guided my sword to success in other contests.

(Exeunt Orestes, Pylades, Electra.)

Chorus

Many indeed are the terrors
the earth breeds, causes for fear;
and the bosom of the deep teems
with monsters repulsive;
overhead hang the lights
that menace in midair;
and all creatures, winged and earthbound,   590
can tell of the wrath of the wind-driven hurricane.
But who shall tell the tale
of man's overbold spirit?
And who can tell how far those passionate loves
can dare, that live in the minds of perverse women,
passions that keep company with man's crazed destruction?
The love passion of the woman, winning victory,
unloving, perverts the coupling companionship
of beasts and men alike.
Let him whose thoughts give him no wings   600
still know, by learning, of dread Althaea's craft,
the device of the burning torch:
she kindled the red brand that was to live
as long as her son, from the moment
he came from his mother,
crying, and made it measure with his life
till it ended in the doom of death.
There again, for your hate, is the story of Scylla,   610
a bloody murderess,
who, on her foes' behalf, destroyed her own kin,
persuaded by the Cretan necklace of wrought gold,
the gift of Minos: plotting malice, she sheared
the immortal hair from Nisus in his deep sleep—

she was a bitch at heart.
And so Hermes took possession of him.
Since I have embarked on the tale   620
of unsavory crimes—what of *this* vile marriage tie
accursed by the house, what of the designs
that the woman crafted against her soldier-husband?
For my part, I honor the hearth unfired by passion,
the spirit of a woman meek and kindly.
But the worst thing told about in any story   630
is the Lemnian deed; with groaning and the spit of contempt
the public voice denounces it. Ever since then,
men speak of what is horrible as "like the Lemnian crime."
The breed of them is gone, dishonored of men,
because God hated them and cursed them,
and no one respects what is hated of God.
In this list of mine, what is wrongly included?
There is a sharp sword, and by the action of Justice,   640
herself trampled under foot unlawfully,
it strikes through and through, near the vitals,
those who violated the majesty of Zeus,
sinning against it all.
Deep-rooted is the trunk of Justice's tree,
and fate forges her sword on her behalf,
and to the house the glorious Fury, deeply brooding,
brings a child at long last to exact
penalty for the pollution of old bloodshed in the past.
                                    (*Enter Orestes and Pylades.*)   650

Orestes
Hello, within there! Do you hear me knocking?
Who is there? Hello, again! Who is at home?
For the last time, come out, do!
if this house of Aegisthus has any hospitality.
                                                (*Enter servant.*)

Servant
Very well; I hear you.
What is your country? Where do you come from?

Orestes

    Take a message to your masters,   660
    to whom I come. I have news for them.
    Hurry, for night's car hastens on to dark,
    and it is time for travelers to cast anchor
    at some house where strangers are welcomed.
    Will someone in authority come out?
    A lady? A man might be better;
    there is a necessary modesty in talking with women
    which blurs what one has to say. One can be franker
    talking man to man; one can deliver clearly
    a clearer message.

                        (Exit servant; enter Clytemnestra.)

Clytemnestra

    Sirs, say what you have to say.
    You shall have all that fits this house to give—
    warm baths, and comfortable beds after your labors,
    and properly respectful faces to tend you.
    If you must deal with matters of greater concern,   670
    that *is* men's business, and I will tell them.

Orestes

    I am Daulieus, a stranger out of Phocis;
    I was going to Argos, on my private business,
    with my own equipment—I am here, as you see me now.
    A man met me as I journeyed, a man unknown to me before,
    as I to him—and asked me about the road
    (his name was Strophius the Phocian, so he told me):
    "If, sir, you are going to Argos in any case,   680
    would you remember, truly, to tell Orestes' parents
    'Orestes is dead'—please
    do not forget this message.
    Whether his friends shall choose to bring him home
    or to leave him here forever a foreigner—
    a permanent resident—bring me back word again
    what their decision is. For now the ribs

of the brazen urn hide the dust of this man much mourned."
I have told you what I heard.
But whether I speak to the masters and his kinfolk,
I do not know. His parents should be told.

Clytemnestra

Ah! Your story tells our utter ruin.   690
Curse of this house, how tough a wrestler
you are against us!
How many things, even safely hidden away,
your watchfulness takes in,
your shafts launched from afar bring down.
You have stripped me of those I loved;
and now Orestes—
he had been wise, he had been taken away
and kept his foot out of destruction's mud.
He was one hope, a healer for the house's craziness,
and now you may cancel the entry in the ledger.

Orestes

I would I could have   700
made the acquaintance of such noble hosts
through happy events, and so been entertained.
What is more agreeable than guest and host
in mutual entertainment!
But my mind scrupled at not completing this thing
for friends, once I had promised and pledged my word.

Clytemnestra

You will be treated with just as much dignity,
you will be just as good a friend to the house.
If you had not, another would have come and given the news.
But now it's time that strangers who have endured   710
the long day's travel should have suitable welcome.

                                        (*To a servant.*)

Here, bring this man to the men's guest chambers;
bring in also his servants and fellow travelers.
And there let them be given the comforts of this house.

I bid you do this as you shall answer it.
We ourselves will give your message to
the master of the house,
and with friends—which we have in plenty—
we will take counsel about this mischance.

(Exeunt all but Chorus.)

Chorus

You dear girls, servants of this house,   720
when shall we show
the strength of our voices for Orestes?
O sacred land, o sacred eminence,
this tomb, where our king lies, that led the fleet,
now hear our words, now come to our help;
for now is the time for crafty Persuasion
to support our side, for Hermes of the Underworld,
a nightly presence, to watch, to preside
over our deadly conflicts of the sword.
The stranger is like one that contrives mischief.

(Enter nurse.)

But here I see Orestes' nurse in tears.   730
Where are you going, Cilissa, out of doors?
The grief that goes with you is no hired mourning.

Nurse

The mistress bade me call Aegisthus speedily
to meet these strangers, that as man to man
he may come and understand this news of theirs.
To the servants she shows a solemn face of sorrow,
but behind the eyes there is a lurking smile
in honor of events that have turned out well—
for her—but for the house a sheer disaster,
in the message that the strangers bring—so clearly.
He surely too will hear and will rejoice   740
when he has grasped the story. Ah me! Ah me!
So much has happened in the past to the house
that was hard to bear—a mingled draught of sorrow

that made my heart in my breast an agony.
But never did I endure the like of this;
all the rest of the cup I have drained with patience,
but my Orestes, my life's work,
whom I took from his mother's hand and raised him up!
My nights broken with his crying, all the many   750
tasks so uselessly performed—I bore them all;
for a baby is so helpless; you must tend him like an animal,
the nurse's mind instead of his own; swaddled,
it does not say what ails it—hunger or thirst
or a wet diaper—the child's young belly
is autonomous! I was the prophet
of his needs, but often deceived, you may be sure,
and so the laundress that made all white again;
a nurse is often nurse and cleaner both,
and *I* doubled in both trades, as I took Orestes   760
to raise as his father's heir. And now I hear
he is dead—O my God!
And I go to fetch this man, this very infection
of our house. He will be right glad to hear the news.
Chorus
You say she bade him come to her. But how?
Nurse
What do you mean by "how"? I don't understand.
Chorus
Was he to come with his retinue or on his own?
Nurse
She bade him bring his personal guards with him.
Chorus
Tell our cursed master nothing of the sort;   770
tell him to come by himself, without a fear,
and listen; tell him to come quickly, gladly.
For a messenger may straighten out a crooked signal.
Nurse
Are you a friend to this our present news?

Chorus

   Yes, but what if Zeus means to change
   our present ill weather?

Nurse

   How can that be? The house's hope, Orestes, is gone.

Chorus

   Not yet. Only a bad prophet would read it so.

Nurse

   What! Do you have news different from what is said?

Chorus

   Go, give your message; do what your mistress told you.

Nurse

   I will obey your words and go. 780
   May all be for the best, as the gods will give it!

                                           (*Exit nurse.*)

Chorus

   You, Zeus, father of the heavenly gods,
   grant my prayer: that those who wish to see
   propriety again in the lords of the house
   win good success! All I have spoken is justly spoken;
   O Zeus, protect us.
   Alas! Make our champion winner over his enemies 790
   within the house. When you make him great,
   you shall be repaid, two- and threefold,
   for your graciousness.
   Know that the son of your friend
   is a colt yoked to the chariot of misfortune;
   but you, if you impose a measured pace
   on the running, you keep his rhythm on to safety;
   you will see the reach of the striding
   paces over the plain.
   You temperate gods that haunt 800
   the recesses of the house that delights in wealth,
   hear us;
   with fresh judgment abolish
   the blood of ancient deeds;

let no murder of long ago
breed another sequence in the house.
You that dwell in the great, fair-established
mouth of the cave,
grant the crowning of the house of the hero;
grant that he may see the radiant   810
light of freedom with welcoming eyes
as it comes out of the veil of dark mist.
May Hermes, the child of Maia, as he justly should,
help him; may he give him a fair wind for what he does!
Many blind utterances he brings to light, if he will,
but when he utters obscure speech
he pulls the darkness of night over the eyes,
and by day it is not much clearer.
Then for the deliverance of the house's wealth   820
we shall raise the shout of female voices;
we shall strike up the magic cry, "She sails well!"
My profit shall increase in this,
and ruin no longer encompass my friends.
But do you, when the share of action comes,
bolder, in answer to her cry of "Child!"
cry, "Father!" and bring to pass
a destruction none can blame.
Keep within your breast   830
a heart like that of Perseus,
and with love to some beneath the earth
and to others above, hold the robe against the Gorgon.
Set bloodly destruction within the house,
and with a glance blot out utterly the guilty.
                                              (*Enter Aegisthus.*)
Aegisthus
I was summoned; my wife's message
brought me here. I learn that there is news
which some strangers have brought,
very unpleasant news—the death of Orestes.   840
It will be another bloody grief laid for the house to bear,

a house already bitten by an old wound.
How may I judge that this news is living and true?
Or can it be the terrified tales of women
which leap, winged, in the air, and then die vainly?
What can you tell me of this that is clear to the mind?
Chorus
    Yes, we have heard. But go into the house,
    and make your own inquiry of the strangers.
    There is no strength in messengers
    like the personal inquiry of man to man on the spot.
Aegisthus
    I am very anxious   850
    to see and test the messenger thoroughly—
    whether he was present, beside the man as he died,
    or only said what he knew from a dim rumor.
    I am wide awake; I will not be easily cheated.

                                        (Exit Aegisthus.)

Chorus
    Zeus, Zeus, what shall I say, from where begin
    with prayers and invocations?
    How can I find words to express
    the loyalty I feel?
    For now the befouled points   860
    of knives that butcher men
    will either achieve the eternal ruin
    of Agamemnon's house,
    or there shall be one that kindles
    the fire and light in freedom's honor,
    and will rule throughout the city;
    he shall have the great wealth of his fathers.
    It shall be Orestes, the beloved of God,
    Orestes, that always as the third against the two
    shall lock in conflict. May it be for victory!
Aegisthus (offstage)
    Oh! Oh!

Chorus
    1. O my God!   870
    2. What is it? How has it ended?
    3. Let us hold off, as the thing is being finished,
    that we may appear guiltless of the evil,
    for now the end of the battle is here.

                                 (Enter servant.)

Servant
    O sorrow, sorrow! Our master is killed.
    Sorrow again, the third cry of lament.
    Aegisthus is no more. Open the doors, I say, and hurry.
    Pull the bolts back from the women's quarters.
    It needs a strong young man to be able for that—
    but hardly strong enough to help the dead.
    That cannot be.   880
    Oh! Oh!
    It is the deaf I speak to; surely they sleep,
    to whom I cry so unavailingly! Where is Clytemnestra?
    My cry has no effect.
    What is she doing?
    It seems that now *her* neck is on the block
    to fall, as she has deserved it should.

                             (Enter Clytemnestra.)

Clytemnestra
    What is this? What does your shouting mean?
Servant
    It is, I tell you, the dead killing the living.
Clytemnestra
    I understand the truth of your riddle.
    We killed by cunning; now we die by cunning.
    Here, someone, quick, bring me an ax.
    Let us find out   890
    if we will conquer or ourselves be conquered.
    This is exactly the bad moment I have come to.

                       (Enter Orestes and Pylades.)

Orestes

Yes, it is *you* I seek. *He* has had enough.

Clytemnestra

My God, he is dead—dearest, strongest Aegisthus.

Orestes

You love him, do you? In the same grave you'll lie
along with him. You'll not prove false to him
even in death.

Clytemnestra

Stop, my child. Have some reverence for this breast
which often, sleeping, you milked to your good,
squeezing it with your gums.

Orestes

O Pylades, what shall I do?   900
I cannot kill my mother.

Pylades

Where then will be Apollo's prophecies
spoken by the Pythia, and the sworn compact?
Have everyone as enemy rather than the gods.

Orestes

You win; in my judgment, your advice is good.

                                        (*To Clytemnestra.*)

Follow me, for I mean to kill you beside him.
You rated him in life above my father;
now in death sleep with him. Between the two men,
you love and hate the wrong ones.

Clytemnestra

I raised you and would grow old with you.

Orestes

You killed my father. Would you live with his son?

Clytemnestra

Fate, my child, was a partner in all this.   910

Orestes

And fate it is that brings this death on you.

Clytemnestra

Do you not fear your mother's curses, child?

Orestes

You brought me to birth, and threw me away to ruin.

Clytemnestra

No no! I "threw you away" to a friend's house.

Orestes

I was a free man's son; you sold me shamelessly.

Clytemnestra

What was the price I got for you?

Orestes

I am ashamed to insult you openly with *that*.

Clytemnestra

Then you must speak equally of *his* lechery.

Orestes

Do not taunt the worker, when you sit inside.

Clytemnestra

It is hard for a woman to live without a man.   920

Orestes

It is the man's work that supports
the woman in the house.

Clytemnestra

I see, my child, you mean to kill your mother.

Orestes

It is you who kill yourself, not I who kill you.

Clytemnestra

Watch out; guard yourself against
your mother's furious hounds.

Orestes

If I let you go, shall I not fear
my father's furious hounds?

Clytemnestra

I think I am singing my dirge at the grave's edge,
and that is vain.

Orestes

It is my father's fate has brought your death.

Clytemnestra

This is the snake I brought to birth and suckled.

Orestes

    The fear in your dream was a true prophet; yes.
    You violated in killing; you are
    violated in suffering.   930

                (*Exeunt Orestes, Clytemnestra, Pylades.*)

Chorus

    I do bewail indeed the death of those two.
    But since the brave Orestes has put the coping stone
    on many bloodlettings, I prefer this end to the other,
    that the eye of this house shall not be lost forever.
    Justice has come at last
    on the children of Priam of Troy.
    Justice has come, and its heavy revenge
    to Agamemnon's house also,
    the double lion, the double war god.
    That banished exile, by Apollo's word,
    has obtained all his destined lot;
    he yielded so prudently
    to what the god told him to do.
    Cry, cry hurrah!   940
    for our ruling house, for escape from its woes,
    for escape from its wastage of wealth
    by two so foul, escape from its past
    of ill luck.
    There has come, too, the god whose concern
    is crafty revenge and a secret fight;
    and the trueborn daughter of Zeus
    took Orestes' hand
    and guided him; rightly we call her
    Justice—apt is the name—
    and the anger she breathes against her enemies
    is pure destruction.
    Even as the Lord Apollo cried   950
    from deep inside his shrine in Parnassus,
    so he struck the corruption, grown ingrained,
    and none can blame him there.

The might of the gods is always master
in action against the wicked.
Worthy it is to worship
the power that supports the heavens.
There is the light for us to see;   960
there the great curb
is taken away from the house.
Arise, O house! For far too long a time
you have lain level with the earth.
Soon time that brings all to accomplishment
shall cross the threshold of the palace,
when from the hearth she banishes
the ruin of infatuation; she has purification to expel it,
and all shall be there to be seen
in smiling-faced fortune;
and we shall cry aloud,   970
"The strangers have fallen! They have vanished
from the palace they tenanted!"
There is light for us to see.
                    (*Enter Orestes and Pylades, with the bodies.*)
Orestes
    See there, the two princes of this land.
    They killed my father, plundered the house.
    They were solemn as they sat on their thrones.
    They are dear friends to one another still—
                        (*He points at the two bodies.*)
    so at least you would think from how they are now.
    Their plighted oath stands fast still, which they swore
    to work the murder of my wretched father
    and die themselves, together.
    Yes, they have kept their oaths well.
    And look you, now, those that have heard
    the sad story,   980
                        (*He holds up an imaginary robe.*)
    look at the traps for my poor father,
    the tyings of his feet,

the fetters of his hands, the linkage of his legs.
Spread the garment out, and show it to all that stand
around here: this was the covering of the man.
Let the father see it—not my father, of course,
but the father that looks down upon
all that is done here, the Sun-Father.
These are the deeds, the filthy deeds, of my mother;
let them be a testimony to Justice, one day,
that this murder which I have done
was justly done; my mother's murder.
(I do not even speak about Aegisthus and his death;
he had what is legally come to him,
the justice due to an adulterer.)
She it was who planned this hateful act upon him,   990
on him whose child she had carried heavy within her,
a child once loved but now, in the event,
a hating enemy.
How does she seem to you? Was she a viper,
or a sea serpent, whose very touch brings corruption
though the hand was not bitten? Shall we so call her,
for her bold and vicious spirit?
What shall I say of the robe? What shall I call it
and make the name good? Was it a snare
for a wild thing, or a covering for a corpse,
a bathrobe for him, trailing to his feet?
No, not a snare, but a net, you might say,
and a robe that fell to his feet.
Maybe the sort of thing a highwayman   1000
might use, to make a living, robbing travelers;
with such equipment he might gladden his heart,
as he plundered many.
May never a woman like her share house of mine!
May the gods curse me rather to have no child!
Chorus (addressing the corpse of Clytemnestra)
    Oh for the wretched act!
    You have ended in pitiful death.

You waited and at the end
retribution flowered.

Orestes

Did she do it, or didn't she?   1010
This robe is my witness
that the sword of Aegisthus stained it.
Time has deepened the stain of murdered blood
that, joining in, has spoiled
the many other dyes in the embroidery.
I praise my father; now I am here to lament him.
You I address, you woven cloth that murdered
my father. Yes, I have pain
for the deed, for the suffering, for our whole race.
I have the pollution, the undesirable
fruits of my victory.

Chorus

No one of all mankind shall cross the end
of his life and know no mischief, nor loss of honor.
Ah me, for this present trouble—and now there is another.

Orestes

I want you to know—   1020
for how it will end I don't know—
it is as if I were driving
a team of horses clear out of the course.
They are bolting with me, they have the better of me!
It is my wits I mean; I cannot control them. There is fear
in my heart that is ready to sing;
I have a dance there under my anger.
So while I am still in my senses I proclaim
to you that are my friends—yes, I confess
I killed my mother, and I did so justly.
She was my father's murderer, a pollution
she was, and one that the gods loathed.
I cite as the chief cure for this awful thing I did—   1030
Apollo and his prophecies.
He spoke to me and said: "If you do this,

you shall be clear of evil blame; neglect it—"
I will not say what punishment he promised;
no one is archer enough to hit the target
of that misery.
And now behold me! Here, I am ready;
with flocks of wool in the garland I will go
to Loxias's shrine, his seat at the navel of the earth,
that which is called the immortal light of fire,
striving to escape the taint of kindred blood.
Apollo bade me seek no other hearth.
In days to come I charge all Argives keep   1040
within their memory how these evils happened,
and bear me testimony, when Menelaus comes.
I myself a wanderer, from this land outcast,
living and dead, leaving my repute to them . . .

Chorus

But what you did was right! Do not unite
your lips to evil utterance; do not blame yourself.
You gave its freedom to all the city of Argos;
you neatly cut off the heads of the two dragons.

Orestes

Oh! Oh!
Can these be women? Look! They are like Gorgons.
Their robes are dark, and they themselves a mass
of writhing snakes! I cannot stand and face them.

Chorus

Your father's dearest son!   1050
What are these visions that torment you?
Stop. Do not fear.
You have won the victory.

Orestes

These are not haunting *visions* of terror;
they are clearly what they are—
my mother's furious hounds.

Chorus

It is the fresh blood on your hand that does it.

It is from this your mind's distraction comes.
Orestes
    O Lord Apollo, how they are crowding in!
    And from their eyes flow streams of loathsome blood!
Chorus
    One cleansing for you only—   1060
    Apollo with a touch
    shall make you free of these torments.
Orestes
    You don't see them; but *I* do.
    I am driven. I cannot stay.

                                          (*Exit Orestes.*)

Chorus
    Good luck go with you! May the god look on you
    with kindly aspect, guarding you throughout
    the perils of the happenings you must meet!
    Here is the third storm
    brought to fulfillment on the royal house,
    savage in its blast.
    In the beginning was the child-eating
    and the sufferings of Thyestes.
    Then, second, came the murder of the king,   1070
    our general-in-chief, cut down in his bath.
    And now the third—Is it a rescuer,
    or must I call him a destruction?
    When will it find completion? When will it end?
    When will the fierceness of our ruin
    fall again to its sleep?

THE EUMENIDES
DRAMATIS PERSONAE

Priestess of Apollo

Orestes

Apollo

Ghost of Clytemnestra

Chorus, the Furies

Athena

THE EUMENIDES

Priestess
 First, in my prayer, I give to Earth first place
 among the gods; first prophetess was she.
 Second, Eternal Law—second was she
 to sit on her mother's oracular seat, as the story goes.
 In third allotment, one more Titan
 daughter of Earth sat there,
 Phoebe—a willing successor, not perforce.
 She gave the oracle to Phoebus,
 a birthday gift—his name, too, echoed hers.
 He left the lake and ridge of Delos
 and beached his ship on the shores of Attica,
 and to this land he came, to his dwelling in Parnassus.
 He was attended and greatly glorified   10
 by the children of Hephaestus. They were his road-makers;
 they made the wild land tame for him. The people
 honored him mightily, as did Delphos also,
 their king and ruler. Zeus seized his mind,
 filled it with god, giving him the art to be
 the prophet, fourth upon this seat of prophecy,
 Apollo, Zeus's spokesman and his son.
 These are the gods with whom my prayer begins.   20
 In my account the primacy is hers,
 Athena of the Fore-Temple; then I reverence
 the nymphs of the Corycian cavern,
 hollow, bird-haunted, the resort of spirits;
 Bromius lives there—I do not forget him—
 from there he led his Bacchanals, as god,
 contriving the death of Pentheus, like snaring a hare.
 I call as well upon the springs of Pleistus,
 and the power of Poseidon,
 and highest and supreme perfecter, Zeus.
 Now as prophet I assume my seat.   30
 Grant that, of all my previous enterings here,

the gods make this the very best.
If there are any Greeks among you,
let them come forward after casting lots,
as is the custom, for I will conduct my prophecies
just as the god prescribes.

> (*She enters and then reemerges, on hands and knees.*)

Horrors to tell! Horrors my eyes have seen!
They drove me from Apollo's house
back out again, so that I have no strength,
nor power to stand; look, I run on my hands,
no quickness in my feet—a terrified old woman
is nothing—indeed, the equal of a child.
I went to the inner shrine,   40
which was covered in garlands; there at the earth's navel
I saw a man, God's stain of guilt upon him,
sitting as suppliant on the very navel stone;
the blood was dripping
from his hands, and his sword was newly drawn;
he wore the olive twigs grown at the treetop,
chastely decked out with lavish flocks of wool,
shining white fleece wool. So far I can speak clearly.
But in front of the man there slept, upon the benches,
a dreadful troop of women.
No, I won't say they were women, but Gorgons;
no, not that, either; their shapes did not seem to me
like Gorgons' shapes.
I saw a picture, once, of those, as they brought   50
the feast for Phineus, but these I saw now
were wingless, black and utterly repulsive.
They snored, the smell of their breaths
was not to be borne,
and from their eyes there trickled a loathsome gum.
The gear upon them was not fit to wear
before God's images, nor within men's houses.
I never saw the tribe like to this company,
nor have I seen the land that could support them

without cause to regret the pain they cost her.
From here on it must be Loxias himself,   60
strong lord of this house,
that should take all this in charge.
He is a healing prophet, and can read portents,
and is, for all other things of this kind,
a force of purification.

(*She leaves; enter Orestes and Apollo.*)

Orestes

O King Apollo, you know not to be unjust;
since you know this, learn not to be neglectful.
Your strength is our best warranty for goodness.

Apollo

I will not desert you; to the end your guardian,
beside you and afar, I shall prove myself
not gentle to your enemies.
Now you see these crazed creatures,
sunk in sleep, its prisoners,
these filthy virgins, ancient, old children;
nor god nor man nor beast will touch them.
Their birth, too, was for evil, for evil darkness   70
is where they live, Tartarus beneath the earth.
They are hated objects of men and the Olympian gods.
I will protect you; but you must flee from them.
Do not spare yourself. For they will hunt you
through all the length of the earth, as you stride onward,
over the ground worn by your feet,
over the seas, and then, over the island cities.
This task of yours will herd you on—do not weary
before it ends; go to the city of Pallas Athena;
there clasp your arms around the ancient image,   80
and sit. In that place we will find judges,
and speeches as our engine to enchant them;
so you shall be freed entirely from your troubles.
Yes, true, I *did* persuade you to kill your mother.
Remember that; do not let fear conquer your mind.

You, Hermes, my blood-brother—
for your father is mine, too—
guard him and be to him, as your title is,
a very escort, a protection;
be his shepherd, for he is my suppliant.   90
Zeus honors the reverence due to outlaws,
with safe conduct to success, however much
they may be outcast by mortal men.

        (*Exeunt Orestes and Apollo; enter Clytemnestra.*)

Clytemnestra's Ghost
  You sleep! Aha! What need have I of sleepers?
Because of you I am so dishonored among
the other dead; those dead that I have killed
never let up their insults against me.
I wander, shamed, among the perished people.
I tell you, I have the greatest blame among them,   100
I that have suffered such outrages from those
dearest to me,
and no god shows his anger on my behalf,
though I was slaughtered by hands that killed their mother.
Look here, look at that wound upon my heart.
For when the mind is asleep, its eyes are bright;
by day men have less vision of what is destined.
You have licked up many of my offerings,
wineless libations, sweet without wine.
To you I used to sacrifice by night
those feasts on the altar, shared with no other god.
Now I see all this trodden underfoot,   110
neglected. He has slipped away, like a fawn,
lightly—even from the closest drawn of nets.
He has escaped, heartily mocking us.
Hear how I plead for my very soul!
Take heed, you goddesses beneath the earth.
For it is I that call you, in a dream,
Clytemnestra.

Chorus (*they whimper like hounds, like dogs dreaming in sleep*)

Clytemnestra
    You would whimper, would you?—
    but the man has escaped, gone far;
    his friends are not at all like mine!
Chorus (*whimpers*)
Clytemnestra
    You are too sleepy; you don't pity me!   120
    Orestes was his mother's murderer,
    and he is fled and gone.
Chorus (*now yelps, with meaningless sounds*)
Clytemnestra
    Yelping, are you, but still sleepy?
    Get up and go!
    What is your destined work, but to bring ill to pass?
Chorus (*sharp yelp*)
Clytemnestra
    Sleep and work-weariness, sworn conspirators,
    have drained the dreadful dragon of her vigor.
Chorus (*the yelping growing more, and sharper*)
    Catch him, catch him, catch him! Mark him down!   130
Clytemnestra
    You are hunting your quarry, but it is in a dream!
    There you give tongue, like a hound true to the scent.
    What are you *doing*? Up now, forget your weariness!
    Do not grow soft in sleep, neglecting my wrongs.
    Let your heart respond to just reproach; to the dutiful,
    such reproaches serve as goads. Direct your bloody breath
    on the man that he
    may wither under its blast, under the belly's fire.
    Follow him, follow him, hunt him again,
    and waste him.
                           (*Exit Clytemnestra.*)
Chorus
    Wake up; you wake her, as I wake you.   140
    What, are you sleepy? Up, kick off your sleep!
    Let us see if what begins now has any meaning.

*(The Chorus here may be variously divided; this is only one guess
of how to do it.)*

1. Ah me, ah me! My friends, we have suffered!
2. I indeed have suffered—and in vain!
We have suffered a hurt most painful,
and evil beyond enduring!
He has slipped from the net; the quarry has gone.
3. Sleep overcame me; I lost my prey.
4. O child of Zeus, what a thief you are.   150
You are young and have ridden down
the ancient gods, through reverence for your suppliant,
a man godless, and bitter foe to his parents.
You are a god, but you stole away
a mother-murderer.
5. Who will say that any of this is just?
From my dream has come a reproach;
it struck me like the driver's whip,
when he grips it in the middle and urges his team;
it struck me below the heart and below the belly.
I can still feel the deadly chill,   160
of the savage public scourge.
6. This is what the new gods do,
who dominate all, overriding justice.
The seat dripping with blood,
hand and foot . . .
You can see earth's navel in blood,
taking on itself a massive curse.
The Prophet has defiled his innermost shrine;   170
the pollution sits at the hearth;
he did it of his own will.
None but himself summoned him to act;
against the law of the gods he has honored the things
of mortal men, and destroyed
what was fated long ago.
Apollo shall have my bitterness,

and Orestes he shall not deliver;
though he flee underground he shall not be free;
defiled, he shall go where he will find
another avenger upon his head.

(*Enter Apollo.*)

Apollo

Out with you! And be quick about it!   180
Go, rid the prophetic sanctuary of your presence,
lest the winged gleaming snake,
sped by the golden bowstring, overtake you!
Then in your agony you will vomit
black foam from your lungs; you will spew out
those lumps of congealed blood you have drawn in.
It is not fit your feet should touch my house here.
You belong where sentences of execution
are carried out, the gouging of eyes,
cutting of throats, castration of young boys,
mutilation, stoning; where the whimperings
of men impaled cry pity.
Do you hear my description   190
of your favorite festival? It fills you with delight
but makes the gods loathe you!
The whole aspect of your shape is a sure guide.
You are such things as ought to haunt the cave
of the blood-gulping lion; you should not rub
your infection off on a nearby oracle.
Be gone, unshepherded by any herdsman!
To such a flock as you, no god feels kindly.

Chorus

My lord Apollo, hear me, in your turn;
you are no joint sharer in these acts;
you are the one main culprit—
you have done everything!

Apollo

How so? Talk long enough to tell me that,   200
no more!

Chorus

You gave an oracle that the stranger
should kill his mother.

Apollo

I gave an oracle that he should
avenge his father. Certainly, I did.

Chorus

And so you promised to accept new blood.

Apollo

And I have bade him to approach this house.

Chorus

—insulting us, who dogged him here.

Apollo

You are not fit to approach a shrine like this.

Chorus

But this is our appointed task.

Apollo

What is this fine appointed task you boast of?

Chorus

We drive from their houses   210
those that kill their mothers.

Apollo

What of the woman who has killed her man?

Chorus

She is no murderer of blood kin with the murdered.

Apollo

So, you would have made of no account, dishonored,
those pledges of Zeus, and of Hera the Perfecter!
In your argument, Aphrodite is discounted utterly—
yet from her the very dearest things come to human kind;
for man and woman, the bed,
when justly kept, their fated bed,
is greater than any oath that can be sworn.
If you give rein to men and women that kill each other,   220
neither visiting them with wrath nor exacting vengeance—
I declare you are unjust to harry Orestes.

For I know you take to heart what the one does,
but neglect the open doings of the other.
The goddess Athena shall oversee this trial.

Chorus

As for this man, I will never let him alone.

Apollo

Pursue him, then; that's so much more work for you!

Chorus

Do not cut down my powers by your words.

Apollo

I would not choose to *have* your powers.

Chorus

Yes, even without them you are counted great,   230
by the throne of almighty Zeus.
But I am drawn by the blood,
the mother's blood, and I will seek due penalty.
I will hunt out this man.

Apollo

But I will come to the rescue of my suppliant;
I will protect him. Terrible is the anger
of a suppliant betrayed, if I should do so willingly,
either among men or gods.
     (*The scene changes to Athens and Athena's temple; enter Orestes.*)

Orestes

Lady Athena, by the command of Apollo
I come; receive me kindly, though I am guilty;
still, my hand's undefiled and unpolluted;
the infection's dull, worn off in other houses
and wanderings among men.
I have crossed over dry land and over sea,   240
keeping Apollo's orders, from his oracle,
and so I approach your house and image, goddess.
Here I watch and wait decision of my case.

Chorus

Enough; here are the man's clear tracks.
Follow the pointings of the voiceless informer against him,

for we trace him out, following blood fresh and clotted,
as a hound does a fawn sorely wounded.
My chest gasps under the stress of many labors,
man-wearying. All earth's expanse
I have haunted. I have come, passing over the sea,
in wingless swoops as fast as any ship.
Now *he* is here, cowering some place or other;   250
the smell of human blood smiles to greet me.
Look, look, look again!
Let your eyes be everywhere,
that he may not give us the slip, and so
be a mother-murderer unpunished.
Here he is! He has twined his hands
round the image of the goddess immortal.
He is seeking protection; he wishes to be
subject to *trial* for what his hands did . . .
But that may *not* be! His mother's blood   260
has fallen to earth; it cannot be recalled.
It was shed and spread on the ground and is gone.

                                    (*To Orestes.*)

But blood to match that blood
you must give me to gulp from your living self,
rich blood-cake from your limbs.
From you I will gain in that horrid draught
fodder for my life.
Living as you are, I will waste you,
and haul you beneath the earth,
that you may pay for your mother's agony
with pains that shall match hers.
And under the earth you shall see those who sinned,   270
that offended god or stranger
or loving parent—all such, each one
shall have what he justly suffers.
For Hades is the great auditor—
under the earth—of mortal men;
he surveys all, written down in the tablets of his mind.

Orestes
I have learned in the school of suffering
and come to know many purifications—when one must speak
and when be silent. In this matter now,
a wise master has instructed me to speak.
For the blood is falling asleep;   280
it is melting off my hand,
and the taint of mother-killing has washed away.
Yes, it *was* fresh once, and at the hearth
of Phoebus Apollo
it was expelled by pig sacrifices.
It would be much too long a story
to tell from the beginning with how many
I have shared company, and they never the worse.
Time, aging, pulls down everything alike.
So now with holy lips I call, in reverence,
Athena, queen of this land, to come and help me.
With never a spear stirred, she will win to her side   290
myself, my country, and my people of Argos,
loyal and dutiful, utterly her allies.
Now, whether Athena is in Libyan country,
or around the stream of Triton where she was born
and sets her foot, upright or draped,
a helper to those she loves; or whether in Phlegra
she looks on the plain like a stout captain of troops—
may she come to *me*
—she's a god and can hear from afar—
To deliver me from evil.

Chorus
No, neither Apollo, nor Athena's strength   300
will rescue you, perishing, uncared for,
knowing in your heart no whereabouts of joy,
the blood sucked from you, fodder for ghosts,
a shade.
Answer me now! Do you despise my words?
You, raised to be mine, a victim sacred to me!

You shall be my feast while still the life is in you,
your throat not cut at the altar. You shall hear
the chant, the chant of the binding chains.
Come join the dance; let us join in it!   310
for we have made our decision
to reveal the song of hatred:
how we, the Furies' regiment,
administer men's fated lives.
We think we are straight in our dealings;
there is no one whose hands are clean,
ever visited by our anger.
Such a one lives his life out uninjured.
But against a sinner like this man,
who keeps secret his murderous hands,
we are upright witnesses for those dead,
exacters of blood in revenge against him—
to that man we appear, in the end.
Mother who bore me, O Mother Night,   320
how we punish those in the dark
and those who still see, oh hear!
For Leto's son has dishonored me,
has stolen this cowering hare of mine,
this thing that is truly sacred to me,
because of his mother's blood.
Over the one to be sacrificed   330
here is our hymn, driving mind askew,
wrenching it from its course,
working its mischief:
This is the Furies' song,
chains on the mind, no sound of the lyre,
it wastes away mortal men.
This is the order for life of the world
that Fate, throughout, has spun
to abide forever:
that for mortal men whose lot was to do
the wanton murder of their own kin—

we shall attend these until
they enter the clay of earth;
and dead, too, such a one,
will not be free too much.
Over the one to be sacrificed   340
here is our hymn, driving mind askew,
wrenching it from its course,
working its mischief:
This is the Furies' song,
chains on the mind, no sound of the lyre,
it wastes away mortal men.
These were the tasks allotted   350
to us on the day we were born—
to keep our hands away from the deathless gods,
that none of *them* shall have feasts with us,
that we shall have neither scot nor lot
in the all-white robes.
For houses' overthrow is my choice,
where the *tame* war god kills his own;
hot in pursuit of that criminal,
however mighty he is, we will quench him
beneath the tide of new blood.
It is our aim to save other powers   360
from these concerns of ours,
and by our prayers to make sure
that none of the gods shall meddle with this,
nor come to dispute it with us.
But to Zeus we are a blood-dripping breed
against whom hatred is just;
he will have no discourse with us.
For houses' overthrow is my choice,
where the *tame* war god kills his own;
hot in pursuit of that criminal,
however mighty he is, we will quench him
beneath the tide of new blood.
Men's good reports are solemn indeed   370

when the reports live under the sky,
but they waste away, and their honor dies,
under the earth,
before the charge of our black robes,
and the dancing pounding of hating feet.
I leapt on high and came crashing down;
I brought all the weight of my foot to bear.
They ran their fastest, but I tripped up
their limbs in distracted ruin.
He falls and knows not his fall;
for the mischief has stolen his mind away,
so thick a mist of pollution
has spread all over him.
He is now a story men tell in sorrow
of a house beset by a thick dark fog.
I leapt on high and came crashing down;   380
I brought all the weight of my foot to bear.
They ran their fastest, but I tripped up
their limbs in distracted ruin.
It all abides; we are the contrivers,
the perfecters of evil, keen-memoried,
holy, inaccessible to mortal prayers.
We follow a task dishonored,
a function quite separate from the gods',
under a light that knows no sun;
the ways we follow are difficult roads,
alike for them that still have their eyes
and those who see only darkness.
Who, then, of mortal men,   390
does not reverence, has not feared,
when he hears of the ordinance sanctioned by fate,
given me by gods in perfectness?
There still abides my ancient office;
I have known no demotion, although
it is under the earth where I hold my rank
and dwell in the darkness without sun.

(*Enter Athena.*)

Athena

I have heard a cry from afar,
from Scamander, where I took possession
of land which the leaders and chiefs of the Achaeans
conceded to me, a great share of captured booty,
entirely for myself forever and ever,
a choice gift for the sons of Theseus.
From there I came driving my feet unwearied,   400
wingless, whirling my deep-bosomed aegis,
driving the car to which the eager colts are yoked—
and here I see this company,
new to this land. I am not afraid, but wonder;
I look and wonder. Who can they be? I speak
to all of you—to you, and to the stranger
seated at my image. You there, who are
not like to anything begotten,
neither among goddesses whom the gods have seen   410
nor similar to mortal shape—yet it is wrong
to speak ill to one that meets you without offense;
that is not justice nor the sacred law.

Chorus

Daughter of Zeus, you shall know all, and quickly,
for we are Night's dark children; we are called
the Curses in our places under the earth.

Athena

I know your race and know your titles, too.

Chorus

Then, in a moment, you will know my function.

Athena

I will, if what you have to say is clear.   420

Chorus

We drive from their houses those that murdered others.

Athena

What is the limit of this hunt for the killer?

Chorus

Where joy can never more be part of life.

Athena

Is this the hunt you set upon this man?

Chorus

Yes; he confessed he was his mother's killer.

Athena

Was he not subject to the force of another's anger?

Chorus

What is the force that drives to matricide?

Athena

This is one half of the case; there are two sides.

Chorus

He will not accept an oath, for he'll not give one.

Athena

You want to be *called* just   430
rather than act justly.

Chorus

How so? Instruct me. You are surely wise enough.

Athena

Do not use the matter of the oaths, I tell you,
to win unjustly.

Chorus

Then, try the case, you; give a straight judgment.

Athena

Will the settlement of the case, then, rest with *me*?

Chorus

Why not? We find you worthy,
and those you spring from.

Athena

What have you to say, in turn, stranger, to this?
Tell us your country and your family
and your circumstances; and then fight the case
against their slander of you—that is, if you sit here
confident in justice, beside my hearth, holding my image,

a holy suppliant, as Ixion did.
On all these matters give me a clear answer. 440
Orestes
O Queen Athena:
first, from the last of what you said
I will remove one great concern of yours.
I am not in need of purification; it was not because
I had pollution on my hand that I sat at your image.
I will give you solid evidence of that.
The law is that the blood-guilty must be silent
until, in the presence of a purifier,
the slaughter of young victims stains him with blood.
Long since, at other shrines, I have been so purified, 450
both with victims and with water from running streams.
This care for me, then, you may leave aside.
As for my race, here is what you should know:
I am an Argive; and my father's name—
I am glad you ask it—it is Agamemnon,
the supreme marshal of our forces at sea.
With him you yourself rendered cityless that city
of Ilium, Troy. But he, my father, died,
shamefully, when he came to his own house. My mother,
black-hearted mother, killed him, with cunning nets,
hiding what proclaimed the murder in the bath.
I myself was in exile before this, but I returned 460
and killed my mother—I will not deny it—
killing to quit the killing of my dear father.
Apollo bore his share of the guilt for all this with me,
for to spur me on, he threatened agonies
if I should not act against the guilty murderers.
Whether I did so justly or unjustly,
is now for you to judge.
However I fare, I am in your hands, content.
Athena
This is too great an issue 470
to pronounce judgment for men,

if any think *that* should be done,
nor is it in accordance with sacred law
that I should decide the issue of murder,
where anger is sharp—especially since you
(*she points at Orestes*)
have been in due submission to the law,
have approached my house, a suppliant purified and harmless.
So I would judge you blameless for the city.
But *these* have functions not lightly to be dismissed,
and if the judgment does not go their way,
afterward the poison that drips from their minds
will fall to the ground and be a pestilence
deadly and dark.
So the matter stands.   480
The outcome for both sides—
to let them stay or to send them away—
contains helpless disaster.
But since the case has fallen to me,
I will choose judges of murder
who have proper respect for an oath,
and so I will set up an ordinance forever.
So, now, you (*pointing to both Orestes and the Furies*)
summon witnesses and evidence
as aids to the sworn truth of the case.
I will come again, when I have chosen the best
from among my people to decide on what to do, truly,
without in their hearts infringing their sworn oaths
to the doing of injustice.
Chorus
Here now is an outcome   490
of the new institutions,
if the plea and the crime
of the mother-killer shall prevail.
For, immediately, this act shall fit
all men for easiness of hand.
Besides, there await parents, in days to come,

many a wounding stroke dealt
by their truly begotten children.
For there will be no brooding wrath   500
of the Furies, that watch mankind,
to attend upon such deeds;
to all deadly things I will throw a loose rein.
As one tells another of a neighbor's suffering,
he may hear of ceasing or abatement
of such crimes—but it is all emptiness,
this advice. The cures do not avail.
Let no one struck by such calamity   510
call aloud, using the phrase,
"O Justice, O Throne of the Furies."
This is the kind of pitiful cry
that a father or mother, when the suffering is fresh,
will utter, when the house of Justice
comes crashing down.
There is a place where terror is good;
it should sit and watch over the mind.
Wisdom comes through   520
the cramping of limits.
Where there is a man who in light of day
fears nothing in his heart;
where there is a city of such men—which men, what city,
fears Justice as once they did?
Do not praise
the life anarchic
nor the life ruled by a master.
God has granted   530
the supremacy in everything
to the mean
between the two; though in his overseeing
he inclines now this way, now that.
The word I speak is a balanced word.
Arrogance is truly the child
of impiety, and from health of mind

comes that well-being which all men love
and all men pray for.
I say it all, when I say:
reverence the altar of Justice;
do not when you see gain, 540
kick that altar aside,
spurning it with your foot that knows not God.
For there shall be a penalty set on that—
the end remains fixed.
So let a man give heedful respect
to the reverence due to parents,
and to the honored comings and goings
of strangers within the house.
Let him be careful of them, too.
The man who is willingly just, 550
under no force of compulsion,
shall not fail of well-being;
no total destruction shall ever attend him.
But I say of the sinner who sets his boldness
in opposition, who carries a load
piled high in confusion,
won with injustice and violence,
to him the day will come
when he pulls down his sail, when the mast cracks
and his ship labors.
He cannot cope with the whirling eddies.
He calls on them that hear nothing.
The God has his laugh at that bold spirit, 560
when he sees him crippled in hopeless pain,
that he never thought would be his.
He cannot breast the waves.
At last he has foundered his early well-being
on the reef of Justice.
None are at hand to see him die
nor give him a tear of pity.

Athena

    Make your announcement, herald,

    and keep back the throng.

    Let the clear Etruscan trumpet, filled with man's breath,

    proclaim to the crowd its sharp-tongued message.

    While the council chamber is filling, it helps   570

    to have silence, to have the whole city

    observe my laws, and for these two

    to have their case well decided.

Chorus

    My Lord Apollo, rule in those matters

    that belong to you;

    tell me, what have you to do with this?

Athena

    I have come

    to give witness; this man in process of law

    is my suppliant, and as such sits in my house,

    and it is I have purified him of murder.

    So I will be his advocate, for I too have the blame

    for his mother's murder.

                         (He speaks to Athena.)

    Introduce the case and judge it,   580

    according to your knowledge.

Athena (to the Furies)

    It is for you to make your speech.

    I declare the proceedings open.

    The prosecutor should speak first; that way

    he may properly inform us of the matter.

Chorus

    We are many, but we will speak in short compass.

                             (To Orestes.)

    Answer us, in turn, after each question:

    First, declare whether you *did* kill your mother.

Orestes

    Yes, I killed her. I do not deny that.

Chorus
There is one of the three wrestling falls already.
Orestes
I am not yet on the ground   590
for you to boast over me.
Chorus
Very well; then tell us how you killed her.
Orestes
I will; with sword in hand I cut her throat.
Chorus
At whose incentive and by whose plans?
Orestes
By Apollo's oracles; he is here, my witness.
Chorus
The prophet instructed you to kill your mother?
Orestes
Yes, and so far I do not fault what has happened.
Chorus
You will, however, if the vote condemns you.
Orestes
— I have my trust; from the grave my father will help me.
Chorus
You trust the dead—when you have killed your mother!
Orestes
Yes, for she was stained   600
with double blood-guiltiness.
Chorus
How was that? Inform your judges here.
Orestes
She killed, in the same man,
her husband and my father.
Chorus
But you are alive—and she now quit of the murder!
Orestes
Why did you not hunt *her* to banishment
when she was alive?

Chorus
Because she was no blood kin to him she killed.
Orestes
I am blood kin, then, to my mother?
Chorus
How else did she raise you, murderer, in her womb?
Your dearest blood tie, to your mother, do you disown it?
Orestes
Apollo, now bear witness, now expose   610
how I have killed her justly. For the action,
as action, I will not deny.
Whether this bloodshed is in your eyes just or unjust,
do you now judge, that I may tell it to these
(*pointing to the jury*).
Apollo
I will speak to *you* (*he motions to the whole assembly*),
this great court of Athens.
I will speak justly, for I am a prophet and will not lie.
Upon my prophet's throne
I never yet spoke of man or woman or city
a word that was not bidden me by Zeus,
father of the Olympians. Be advised
how strong that justice is; I bid you follow his will.
There is no oath stronger than Zeus.   620
Chorus
Zeus, you say, Zeus gave you this oracle
to tell Orestes here that in avenging
his father's murder he should forever dishonor his mother!
Apollo
It is not the same for a nobleman to die—
honored with the scepter, which the gods give princes—
as to die by a woman's hand, not with furious arrows
launched by an Amazon, from afar, but, as you will hear—
you, Pallas Athena, and you who have your seats
to make your votes decide upon this matter.
He had come from war where he had fared   630

for the most part well; he was received with loyalty;
then as he went through his bath and she enfolded him,
at the end, with a robe, and had him fettered
in those embroidered folds, she struck him down.
This which I now have told you was the end
of majesty and the great fleet's commander.
Such was this woman; so I have described her,
to move the people appointed to judge the case.

Chorus

According to your story, Zeus gives precedence   640
to the fate of a father, but he himself
fettered his father, ancient Cronos. How
does your account, then, fail to be inconsistent?
I call the judges to witness, to hear this.

Apollo

You loathsome creatures, hated by the gods,
one may break *fetters*—there are cures for that—
and expiation is often a potent engine.
But when the dust has snatched to itself the blood
of a man once dead, there is no resurrection.
My father has made no spells for *that;* all other things
effortlessly he turns now this way and now that.

Chorus

Look to how you defend acquittal of this man.   650
He has shed on the ground his mother's blood—
will he then live in his father's house in Argos?
What public altars will he use? What lustration
of brothers will receive him?

Apollo

This I will tell you; mark how clear my words.
She that is called the mother of the child
is not its parent, but the nurse of the new seed;
it is the stallion's thrust that is the parent;   660
the woman saves the young living plant for a stranger,
as she is a stranger to him, saves it among those
couples whom the gods do not blight with stillbirth.

I will give you proof of what I say; a father
may generate without a mother; see—
here is at hand my witness—the child of Olympian Zeus.
She never lay in the womb's dark recesses;
she is a living plant, such as no goddess could bear.
Pallas, as I know all other things,
I will make your city and your people great,
and so I sent this man to sit in your house
that there might be trust between you always,
that you might have him as your ally, goddess,
and those his children in the days to come;
and so it be forever and forever   670
a faithful covenant of both your peoples.

Athena

Am I now to bid the judges in all honesty
give a true judgment? Has enough been said?

Chorus

We have shot our bolt altogether. I remain
to hear how the decision shall be made.

Athena (speaking to the jury)

Now, how shall I act to be clear of blame from you?

Apollo

You have heard what you have heard;
in the truth of your hearts,
sirs, give your votes—
and respect the oaths you have sworn.

Athena

Here is my ruling now, you men of Athens: 680
you who judge this first trial of bloodshed.
This shall be for all time to come for the people of Aegeus
the judges' council chamber.
For this is Ares' hill, place of the Amazons;
here their tents stood when they came here campaigning
in hatred against Theseus; here they built
tower against tower, a new city against the City.
They sacrificed to Ares, and the rock

and crag was hence called Areopagus.
Here is the city's Reverence, and her brother, Fear,   690
shall check among the citizens injustice
night and day alike, providing that they
do not themselves make innovation
with influx of mischief on the laws. Pure water—
foul it with mud, you will never have it to drink.
My counsel to you citizens is this:
do not set amongst you for your honor
either anarchy or a master's rule.
Do not cast terror utterly
out of your city; for what man is just
that has no fear of anything?
If the citizens   700
fear what they honor, justly, they shall have
a saving fortress in their land and city
such as no other people of mankind
possess, neither among the Scythians
nor those in Pelops's country.
This shall be a council chamber untouched by gain,
revered, high-spirited, a true guard
over your land, watchful for those who sleep.
As such I shall create it.
At this length I advise my citizens
for days to come; for *now,* be upright,
bear your vote and decide the case
with reverence for your oath. My speech is done.

(*They cast their votes.*)

Chorus
    Yes, I shall give you counsel; do not dishonor   710
    this company of ours; we can be dangerous.
Apollo
    And I bid you fear those oracles
    that are both mine and Zeus's; let them not be fruitless.
Chorus (*to Apollo*)
    Bloodshed is not your function,

but you honor it.
Henceforth the oracles you give will be impure.
Apollo
And so my father stumbled in his judgment when
Ixion, the first murderer, made his appeal?
Chorus
You may have your say, but if I lose the case,
I will be a danger to this land henceforth.
Apollo
Neither among the gods that are new or old   720
do you find honor. I shall win over you.
Chorus
Just such a thing you did in Pheres' house,
persuading the Fates to make a *man* immortal.
Apollo
Is it not just to benefit a worshiper,
especially when he is in greatest need?
Chorus
You destroyed all the old ways of the world
when you made drunk and cheated the old goddesses.
Apollo
You will not win the settlement of this case,
and then will you vomit your poison,
but it will not hurt those you hate.
Chorus
You have ridden me down, young god as I am old.   730
I wait to hear the settlement.
I have two minds still about my hate for the city.
✓ *Athena*
It is my task to render final judgment:
this vote which I possess
I will give on Orestes' side.
For no mother had a part in *my* birth;
I am entirely for the male, with all my heart,
except in marriage; I am entirely my father's.
I will never give precedence in honor

to a woman who killed her man, the guardian of her house.
So if the votes are but equal, Orestes wins.   740
Let the judges now proceed
to cast out the votes from the urns that contain them.

Orestes

O Phoebus Apollo, how will the decision go?

Chorus

O Night, dark Mother, are you watching?

Orestes

For me, it is death by hanging, or the light of life.

Chorus

For us, destruction or continued honor.

Apollo

Count out the thrown votes, sirs;
be careful not to wrong anyone in sorting them out.
One missed decision can mean a great mischief;   750
one vote cast often saves a house.

                                                    (*Silence.*)

Athena

The man has been acquitted in the murder suit,
for the number of the votes is equal.

Orestes

Pallas, you have saved my house.
I that had lost a fatherland am restored to my house
by you. Truly, some Greek will say,
"There is an Argive who once again is home
in all his father owned, thanks to *them,*
Athena and Apollo and that Third,
the Savior who rules all."
He it was who out of regard for my father's death   760
saved me, when he saw these as my mother's advocates.
Now I shall go to my home again, but first
I shall pledge my oath to this land and to this people
for all the multiplying time to come,
that never shall a prince of Argos come
to raise an enemy's spear against your country.

On that day shall ourselves be in the grave
but against those who contravene this oath
we shall loose mischief that will cripple them,
make their wayfarings desperate and their journeys
full of ill omen, that they shall repent
of what they strove to do.
But if they keep our covenant and honor   770
this city of Pallas, with their spears as allies,
we shall be all the kinder to them, ourselves.
Farewell then, goddess, and governors of this city,
may all your struggles show no enemy escaping,
but safety to yourselves and victory always.

Chorus

O you young gods, you have ridden down
the old ways; you have snatched them out of my hands.
I have no more honor, but in my wretchedness   780
my anger will be heavy; on this land
I will relieve my heart's pain, drops on the earth,
poison, overbearing poison.
A blight will come of it—no leaves, no children—
O Justice! The blight will attack the land
and cast upon it infections which kill its people.
Shall I weep? What shall I do?
I am mocked with laughter; among the citizens
I have intolerable sufferings.
O great unlucky daughters of Night,   790
dishonored in your sorrow.

Athena

Let my words prevail on you
not to take this so ill.
You have not been conquered—the suit has truly ended
with equal votes; you have no dishonor in that.
But there was the clearest testimony from Zeus—
he gave the oracles and was himself the witness—
that Orestes should come to no harm from his act.
Will *you* then vomit your dark hate against   800

this land? Reflect; do not rage so, do not
bring infertility upon them, letting fall
the drops of divine hatred, keen cutting edges
that cruelly gnaw the seed away. For I
make an absolute promise to you, in all justice,
of a seat and a hiding place within this country
to be rightly yours, and you may sit at the hearth
on gleaming thrones, and be honored
by all the citizens.

Chorus

O you young gods, you have ridden down
the old ways; you have snatched them out of my hands.
I have no more honor, but in my wretchedness   810
my anger will be heavy; on this land
I will relieve my heart's pain, drops on the earth,
poison, overbearing poison.
A blight will come of it—no leaves, no children—
O Justice! The blight will attack the land
and cast upon it infections which kill its people.
Shall I weep? What shall I do?
I am mocked with laughter; among the citizens
I have intolerable sufferings.
O great unlucky daughters of Night,   820
dishonored in your sorrow.

Athena

You are *not* dishonored; do not haughtily
ruin this land—you are gods and they are mortal.
I myself trust in Zeus, and—why should I speak of it?—
I am the only one among the gods
that knows the keys of the house wherein is sealed
the lightning bolt—but there's no need of that.
Be persuaded by me; do not pour out   830
vain words against this country, words to bear,
as fruit, a general blight of all who bear fruit,
but lull to sleep the bitter strength of the dark blood;
for you can share my majesty and peace;

you can have the firstfruits of this large land
as sacrifices for children and for marriage;
and when you have these forever, you will say
that I was right.

Chorus

That I should suffer so!
I with my thoughts of ancient times,
that I should dwell beneath the earth,
an unhonored vile thing.
My breath is all anger and malignity.   840
Who assails my body? What pain is in my spirit?
Hear me, Mother Night.
For the ancient honors of the gods
have been snatched away and made nothing of
by cunning treachery.

Athena

I will bear with your moods for you are older,
and though, for that, you are wiser than I,
Zeus has given me, too, a mind to perceive.
If you go to alien nations, I tell you,   850
you will find how much you loved this land,
for the on-flowing course of time shall see more honors
for these my citizens. If you have your place
of honor beside the temple of Erectheus,
you shall have from men and women worshiping
what you will never obtain from any others.
Only, I pray you, in this country of mine
do not cast sharp provocations to draw blood,
making mischief in the hearts of the young,
crazing the wits with never a drop of wine;
nor, as one takes the heart out of fighting cocks,   860
set among my citizens civil war, that turns their courage
against one another. Let there be war indeed—
it will come easily enough—but war outside
in which they shall find their dangerous love of glory.
I do not want my fighting cocks at home.

All this you can have, if you will, from me.
Be good to us, take good from us, take honor
and share with us this land much loved of God.
Chorus

    That I should suffer so! 870
    I with my thoughts of ancient times,
    that I should dwell beneath the earth,
    an unhonored vile thing.
    My breath is all anger and malignity.
    Who assails my body? What pain is in my spirit?
    Hear me, Mother Night.
    For the ancient honors of the gods
    have been snatched away and made nothing of
, by cunning treachery.
Athena

    I will not weary of telling you your benefits, 880
    that you may never say, being old,
    and a goddess, you were dishonored and destroyed
    by me that am younger, and by men, my citizens,
    driven abroad from this our land, an outcast.
    If you find sacred the honor of Persuasion,
    the sweetness of my tongue, its power to charm,
    then remain here with us; if you will not,
    you will be wrong to turn upon my land
    your rage and malignity, or damage
    my people; for you may certainly
    be our land's lord, justly honored for ever.
Chorus

    Lady Athena, what is the home you speak of? 890
Athena

    One free of all unhappiness; only receive the gift.
Chorus

    Suppose I do. What honor continues mine?
Athena

    No household will thrive without you.

Chorus

Will you indeed allow me so much power?

Athena

I shall prosper the enterprises of your worshipers.

Chorus

And you will guarantee this for all time?

Athena

I do not promise what I will not perform.

Chorus

There speaks your enchantment indeed!   900

I give over my anger.

Athena

If you stay here, you will find you gain new friends.

Chorus

What song would you have me chant over this land?

Athena

A song of all that waits upon good victory.

From land and sea and sky may breezes and sunshine

enfold our land. May the earth yield crops

and cattle their offspring in plenty for the citizens,

all flourishing without stint, and all the safety

that goes with multitude of children.

Prosper the enterprises of the pious. I   910

like a good gardener am happy when my plants,

the breed of just men here, know no sorrow.

So may your actions be. For my part,

in warlike contests I will not hold back

until I have honor for this city for victories

throughout the world.

Chorus

I shall accept joint tenancy with Pallas.

I shall not dishonor the city

which Zeus Almighty and the god of war

hold as the guard station of the gods,

the glory of heavenly beings who are Greek.

For this city,   920
I give my prophecy with kind good will,
and I pray that the sun's bright radiance
bring from the earth abundantly
all goods of life that depend on Fortune.

Athena
I have acted out of good will to my citizens
in giving a home here to these divinities,
so great, so dangerous in their displeasure.
These powers have for their allotted function   930
everything in human life.
He who has met them in ill humor
knows not whence the blows assail his life.
For the offences of the ancestors
hale him before Them; his destruction is silent
but grinds him to dust, for all his loud talk,
under the Furies' hatred.

Chorus
May no harmful winds blight your trees—
here is my litany of favor—
may no blinding flame   940
working evil on the plants
cross the frontier of the seasons.
May no disease, destroying the fruitfulness
of the crops, steal darkly upon you.
But let Pan
nourish your prosperous flocks
with twin lambs in due time.
May what the earth brings forth
in richest soil, as the gods' gift,
give of its bounty.

                              (*Athena turns to the citizens.*)

Athena
Do you hear this,
you that are the city's guardians?
What consummation of good!   950

For great is the power of the dread Fury,
amongst the immortals and also beneath the earth;
and amongst men, especially,
they bring to perfection for all to see
what they have provided:
for some, occasions for song;
for others, a life rich in tears.

Chorus

The chances that bring about men's deaths
before their time—
may nothing such be yours!
You goddesses, the Fates,   960
my mother's sisters, grant—
yours is the power—
that young girls ripe for love
will find the men for their lives.
You are the upright-dealing spirits
that have a part in every home,
that bear a weight in every time,
most honored among every one of the gods,
where the just dwell together.

Athena

That you bring such good to fulfillment
for my country, out of your kindness,
I am heartily glad.
The face of Persuasion I revere   970
because she looked upon
my tongue and mouth, as I spoke against
these, who were then angry and rejecting;
but Zeus of the Assembly was victorious,
and the victory we won was in the contest
for blessings for all time.

Chorus

This is my prayer:
that never in this city shall stir the noise
of faction, that is never sated with evils.

May the dust never drink the black blood   980
of fellow citizens, in their lust for revenge,
hunting for murder to answer murder,
to the ruin of the city.
Rather let them give joy for joy
in harmony, a community united.
Let them hate, too, with one mind—
for among mankind, this, too, cures much.

Athena

How minded are they to find the road
of a gracious tongue!
From these fearful countenances   990
I see great blessing come to my citizens;
for if you kindly honor the Kindly Ones,
always and greatly honor them,
you shall live for all time
with land and city straight in its justice—
and all shall see it as such.

Chorus

Farewell to you in the wealth that is your right!
Farewell, you people of this town,
that sit near Zeus, loved by
the Maiden Goddess who is loved.
You are wise   1000
in the course of time.
The Father reveres
those that shelter under her wings.

Athena

Farewell to you, too. I must go before you
to show you your palace, in the sacred light
of your escort of worshipers.
Hasten to your place under the earth
attended by solemn sacrifices.
Keep away, restrain all destruction,
but send to our city all profit
for victory.

(*Athena turns to the second chorus, a band of citizens that lead the*
Furies to their new home.)

Guide them on their way,   1010
you citizens, children of Cranaus;
guide these Powers that will settle among you.
And good among the citizens be the thought
that attends upon good received.

Chorus

Farewell, farewell again—I say it twice—
all you of this city,
Heavenly Ones and mortal men
that live in the city of Pallas.
While you show piety
for my sharing in your lives
you shall find fault with nothing that befalls you.

Athena

I praise you for the meanings of your prayers   1020
I shall send you on your way with light
of radiant torches to those places
underneath, beneath our earth. Your escort
will be those who guard my image, a just escort.
For the eye of all this land of Theseus
must come forth, this glorious crowd
of children, wives, and the band of elder women.
With clothes of scarlet dye honor them,
and let the light of fire set them on the road,
that this kindly company, favoring us, shall show
for time to come, gallantry in our sons.

The escort

Advance, in order, great and venerable,   1030
you virgin daughters of Night.
This is your loyal escort.
Hush, holy silence, all you who attend.
Beneath the ancient caverns of the earth,
be glorified, in honor, in sacrifice, and in Fortune.
Hush, holy silence, all the people.

In graciousness and in just thought   1040
for our land, come hither, Holy Ones,
rejoicing on your road with torches eaten by flame.
Now, now, sing in songs of praise.
Peace be forever on the houses and citizens of Athens.
For Zeus who Sees All and the Fates
on these terms have come together.
Now, now, sing in songs of praise.

PART TWO
ACTING VERSION

AGAMEMNON

Sentry

You gods, release me.
Crouched like a dog, I watch always, all year long,
on the tower of the sons of Atreus.
I have come to know the nightly gathering of the stars.
They bring the seasons and the changes of the seasons;
but for me, no change.
It is a different flaming light I watch for—
the beacon fire, the tell-tale witness that Troy is captured.
Such are my orders, orders from a hopeful queen
who thinks with the mind of a man.

I have a bed here, soaked with dew, always shifting.
But no dreams. Fear is my visitor, not sleep.
I cannot close my eyes for fear.
Sometimes I whistle or hum;
I try that way not to sleep.
And then the sorrow comes.
This house is in bitter trouble.
Once it was well governed; not now.
Still, if the fire of the good news shines through the darkness,
all our troubles may be over.

The beacon! Day out of night!
My lady, Agamemnon's wife, get out of bed!
Cry aloud a blessing on this beacon,
since Troy is surely captured.
I will myself begin the dance.
Oh, that I could touch with this hand of mine
the hand that I love, my lord's.

As for the rest, I haven't a word;
a great ox stands on my tongue.
If the house itself had a voice to speak,

it would tell the clearest story.
I choose to speak to those who understand;
for the others, I am all forgetfulness.

Chorus

This is the tenth year
since they launched from this land
the Greek fleet of a thousand ships
to help right wrongs done.
They launched it, King Menelaus,
great plaintiff against Priam,
and Agamemnon, his brother.

From their hearts the great war cry;
they screamed like eagles,
in lonely agony for the loss of their nestlings.

But One yet higher up, some Apollo or Pan or Zeus,
Zeus god of guest-friends,
sends the sons of Atreus against Paris;
in this quarrel over a woman of many men,
he would lay upon Greeks and Trojans alike
many wrestlings where the limbs grow heavy
and the knee is pressed into the dust.
Yet it is now as it is.
Fulfillment moves toward what is fated.
And not with burnt offerings nor with pouring on of wine
nor sacrifice to the gods below
will you assuage that stubborn anger.

But we, dishonored for the ancientness of our flesh,
were left behind then when the army went;
we remain, propping on staffs a strength like a child's.
For the child's marrow, too, leaps within his breast
but is only the match of an old man's;

the god of war is not there either.
And the overold, the leafage already withering,
walks his three-footed way, no stronger than a child;
wanders, a dream in the daylight.

What is the matter? What is the news? What have you heard?
What message do you trust, that you order sacrifices
at all the altars?
Cure this care that now broods darkly on our minds.
I tell how Agamemnon and Menelaus, the sons of Atreus,
twin-throned, single-hearted
lords of the youth of Greece,
were sent against the land of Troy
with spear in hand to exact vengeance
for the rape of Helen.
The furious omen-birds sent them,
one black eagle, one white-tail,
the kings of birds to the kings of the ships.
Near the palace they came, and where all could see them,
they fed on the unborn young of the pregnant hare,
mother and all, pulled down in the hare's last flight.
Cry sorrow, sorrow, but let the good prevail.

Calchas, the honest prophet of the army
knew the princely leaders and hare-devourers—
knew that they were one and the same.
And so he declared in his prophecy:
"In time, this journey will capture Troy, Priam's city;
and all the herds that graze before her towers
shall Fate give violently to plunder.
I only pray that no anger from the God will cast a cloud
upon this army forged to be
a great iron bit in the mouth of Troy.
For Queen Artemis hates those winged hounds
who devour the mother hare with her brood

before they come to birth.
She hates the eagles' feast.
Cry sorrow, sorrow, but let the good prevail.
I call on Apollo the Healer
to keep Queen Artemis from setting against the Greeks
those contrary winds, staying winds,
winds that stop sailing altogether.
She might do this in eagerness for a different sacrifice,
the sacrifice of a daughter, that is lawless and horrible.
Full of terrors it lurks, long-memoried,
an anger that punishes child-slaughter."

Such were the prophecies of Calchas's voice;
cry sorrow, sorrow, but let the good prevail.

Zeus, whoever he is,
if it is dear to him to be so called,
this is how I call him.
There is only Zeus.

Zeus it is who has laid down the rule
that understanding comes through suffering.
Instead of sleep there drips before the heart
the recollected sorrow of past pain.
It is against our wills that we become wise.

So on that day, Agamemnon, leader of the Greek ships,
caught his breath at his sudden calamity,
for a hurricane that came from Strymon
caused deadly delays, starvation.
It wore down the flower of the Greeks.
So when the prophet's voice rang out,
proclaiming the other, heavier cure for the bitter storm,
the sacrifice of a daughter,
the sons of Atreus beat the ground with their staves
and could not hold back their tears.

Then Agamemnon spoke and said,
"Heavy indeed my fate if I disobey,
but heavy, too, if I must butcher my child,
the glory of my house."

When he put on the harness of Necessity,
his spirit veered in a breath of change—
to impiety, unholiness, desecration,
and from it he drew audacity for his heart
to stop at nothing.
For indeed there is a wretched distraction of the wits,
a primal source of ruin,
that puts recklessness in man's mind
and counsels ugliness.
So he dared to become his daughter's sacrificer
to aid the war waged for a woman.

Her prayers, her cries of "Father," her maiden life,
they set at nothing.
Agamemnon ordered his servants to lift her
carefully over the altar
after the prayer, swooning, her clothes all round her,
like a young goat, a gag on her beautiful lips.
She stood out, like a figure in a picture, struggling to speak.

What happened after that I neither saw nor tell.
But the scales of justice have come down and brought
with suffering, understanding.
You will learn the future when it happens.
Till then, let it be.

(Enter Clytemnestra.)

Is it in the hope of happy news
that you are ordering sacrifice?

Clytemnestra
    As the proverb goes,

"May dawn be the dawn of good news
as she comes from her mother night"—
you shall learn of a joy greater than you hope.
For the Argives have captured Priam's city.
Chorus
What? I cannot believe you; I cannot understand.
Clytemnestra
Troy is the Greeks' city now.
Are my words clear?
Chorus
Joy steals over me, and calls out tears, too.
Clytemnestra
Your eyes proclaim you a subject true and loyal.
Chorus
What makes you trust the news? Have you proof of it?
Clytemnestra
I have, of course—unless the gods deceived me.
Chorus
But when was it that the city was sacked?
Clytemnestra
In this last night that brought this dawn to birth.
Chorus
What messenger can be as quick as that?
Clytemnestra
The god of fire, sending his brilliant glow from Mount Ida.
Beacon sent beacon here with courier fires,
Ida to the crag of Hermes in Lemnos;
then from that island a third flame sent on
to the heights of Athos that belong to Zeus;
and high, spanning the sea's back,
the pine fire sent its golden blaze, almost a sun,
to the watchtowers of Macistus.
They in their turn lit up and sent the message farther,
firing a great heap of ancient gorse.
The beacon's light never flagged,
but leapt over the plain of Asopus like a radiant moon,

to Mount Cithaeron, then launched its light
over the Gorgon lake; and coming to
the goat-haunted mountain,
a huge beard of flame that burnt ungrudgingly,
over the Saronic gulf, now become its mirror,
beyond the headland, till it struck the heights of Arachnus,
and then again
struck right here on this roof of the sons of Atreus—
this fire that is the grandchild of that fire on Mount Ida.
Such proof I have and such confirmation,
sent me out of Troy by my man.

Chorus
   My lady, to the gods once again
   I shall give my prayer of thanks,
   but I would like you to tell me all this again,
   that I might hear the words and marvel at them
   from beginning to end.
Clytemnestra
   Troy is captured; this is the day; the Greeks hold it.
   Within that city there rings out
   a volume of cries that do not mingle.
   This is how I see it.
   Mix oil and vinegar in the same jar
   and you could not call them friends.
   So in Troy you might hear two sorts of crying:
   the conquered and the conquerors.
   The act is single, the meaning double.
   Here are these:
   throwing themselves on the dead bodies
   of husbands and brothers,
   children on the bodies of their fathers,
   all sorrowing for the destiny of their dead,
   they cry from throats no longer free.
   Then there are the others:
   they are already living in Troy's captured houses,

free of the frost beneath the sky, free of the dews.
They will sleep all night long without a guard,
like happy men.
If they revere the gods of that city in that captured land,
if they revere the gods' sacred places,
they who are conquerors will not be reconquered.
Only let no lust seize the army first,
let no greed conquer them,
to make them ravish what they should not.
They must still make the home voyage safely,
travel the other leg of the double track.
But even if the army came through offenseless
in the sight of the gods,
the wrong done to the dead may yet awaken.
This is what you hear from me, a woman.

Chorus

My lady, you talk wisely, like a sensible man.
Surely we should thank the gods
for what they have done for us.

O Zeus the king, you that have cast upon the towers of Troy
a close-fitting mesh so that no one young or old
can overleap the great net of slavery,
great Zeus of guest-friends I revere.
Zeus has done all this. He has forever bent his bow
against Paris.
Zeus has acted as he has determined.
The black grain in Paris shows through the test,
like base copper rubbed bare with use.
He has been like a child that chases a bird;
he has brought on this city an intolerable infection,
and no one of the gods will hear his prayer.
Paris, who came
to the house of the sons of Atreus
and stained with shame the table of his host
by the theft of that host's wife, Helen.

Helen has left to her fellow citizens
the clanging of shields, the arming of sailors, ambushes.
To Troy she has brought ruin instead of dowry.
For those who left the land of Greece,
in the house of every one of these
there is grief that reaches the heart.
They know whom they have sent forth, but instead of men
there come home urns and ashes to each house.

The war god is a money changer; men's bodies are his money.
He holds the scales in the battle of the spear.
From Troy he sends back to those who loved them
the scrapings of dust made heavy with their tears;
he loads the elegant urns with the dust that was once a man.
They mourn this man as they praise him—
how skilled he was in the fight—and another—
how gallantly he fell in his blood—
for another man's woman.
That is their whispered snarl.
But those others—the dead—
keep to their graves in all their beauty,
where they were, around the walls of Troy.
The enemy land that they have taken at last
has taken them, hidden them in itself.

(*Enter a herald.*)

Herald
    O my fathers' earth, Argos, Argos,
ten long years and I have come to you.
I never dreamed that I would have for my share in death
a piece of dearest Argive land.
Now welcome earth, welcome the light of sun,
and Zeus supreme lord.
Welcome back what's left of us after the fight.
Receive now with faces bright in joy—
now receive the king in glory after so long,
King Agamemnon.

Give him true welcome,
the king who dug down Troy with the spade of God's justice,
made plowland of Troy;
and the seed has perished from all their country.
Their altars and the shrines of their gods are gone.
Such a yoking chain has he cast on Troy,
the king, Atreus's son, the old and happy man.

Chorus
Herald of the Argive army, joy on your homecoming!
Herald
Joy indeed. If the gods should end my life now,
I'd not deny them.
Chorus
Has the love of your lost homeland tortured you so?
Herald
Yes; the tears you see are tears of joy.
Chorus
But you got love for the love you gave.
Herald
You mean this land has missed the army as we missed you?
Chorus
We were faint and weak and so have groaned for you.
Herald
Why so uneasy? What horror was in your mind?
Chorus
I say nothing and am safe—a long, long silence.
Herald
How could that be? Your king was away;
did you fear others?
Chorus
As you said just now, I would have welcomed death.
Herald
It *has* been a success. Of course, in the length of time,
one must say some things have gone well, some ill.

Who except the gods lives the whole span of his life
without trouble?
Yes, if I were to speak of the hard work and the bad quarters,
the narrow gangways and the hard beds,
there's plenty to complain about.
Our beds were under the enemy's walls.
Rain from the sky and dew from the grass soaked us
and kept rotting our clothing
and bred lice in our hair.
And the winter, which killed the birds.
And then there was the heat,
when the sea fell on its noontide bed and slept.
Not a breath of wind, not a stir on the waves—
Oh, why should I still feel pain for all this?
It's over, isn't it, all the trouble?
It's over indeed, for them, too, the dead;
they'll never have to trouble about getting up again.
I'm ready to say a long goodbye to all that's happened.
Those of us who have sped over land and sea
can stand facing the sunlight and make our boast:
"There was a day when the Argive army took Troy."

Clytemnestra
I shall learn the whole story from my lord himself.
What sweeter day for a wife's eye to see
than when she opens the doors to her man
coming from the army,
when the gods have brought him safely back to her?
Tell my husband this:
bid him come as quick as he can,
the city's darling.
When he comes he'll find his wife
true as he left her,
the watchdog of his house,
devoted to him, enemy to his enemies,

the same always and ever.
I never broke the seal
in all those years.
I know of no pleasure with another man
nor any talk or evil gossip against me,
any more than I know how to dip this blade
to temper it.
Such is my boast, so full of truth
that even a well-bred wife
need not blush to utter it.

(*Exit Clytemnestra.*)

Chorus

She has spoken very suitably
for those who understand her.
But tell me, what of Menelaus?
Was he among the returning army?
Is he safe among you?

Herald

I don't know how to put a fair face on lies:
the man has vanished from the Greek army,
he and his ship.
In the night, waves lashed by a storm
arose to plague us.
The Thracian winds battered ship on ship.
In the hurricane and sheets of hail,
they sank from sight.
When the clear light of the day came back,
we saw the sea blooming,
and its flowers were dead Greeks and wrecks.
For ourselves and our ship, we went unharmed;
some god stole us through it or begged us off;
he must have steered us himself,
for no man touched the steering oar.
Luck chose to become our savior, and sat on our ship,

seeing how the fleet had been pounded and ground to pieces.
Let it turn out well.

Chorus

Let it turn out well.

Herald

As for Menelaus,
if the beams of the sun discover him living and seeing
—for surely God will not yet blot out
the whole family—
there is some hope that he'll come home again. Helen!

(*Exit herald.*)

Chorus

Helen! Who can have named her so,
with such truth, utterly?
She was called Helen,
the bride won by the spear, Helen sought in strife.
Helen means death, and death indeed she was,
death to ships and men and city
as she sailed out of the delicate fabrics of her curtained room,
fanned by the breeze of giant Zephyr;
and the man-swarm of shield-bearing hunters
came on the track of her,
the vanished track of the oar blades.
To Troy it drove her,
the wrath that brings fulfillment,
and again the word proved true, that equates
marriage and mourning.
She came to the city of Troy
a spirit of windless calm,
the delicate glory of wealth,
the soft arrow darting from her eyes,
the flower of love that bites the heart.
Zeus the god of guests brought her there,
a Fury to make wives weep.

It is the wicked deed that breeds more wickedness.
For the house that is straight-dealing and just
is fated always to have good children.
For justice shines in houses grimed with smoke,
and she honors the good man.
And those gilded palaces where hands are dirty
she leaves, averting her eyes;
and she guides everything to its due end.

(Enter Agamemnon and Cassandra.)

My lord, conqueror of Troy, descendant of Atreus,
how shall I greet you, how do you reverence,
neither exceeding nor scanting due measure of praise?
When you led the expedition from Greece,
I saw you painted in ugly colors—
I will not hide that from you—
as one who had an unskillful hand
on the rudder of his wits
when you tried to win back through men's dying
a willing whore.
But now from the depth of my heart,
I say, May the work be kind to those who did it so well.
In time you shall know
which of your citizens that stayed here at home
dealt justly, and which did wrong.

Agamemnon

First Argos and my country's gods,
I must address you; you and I are coauthors
of my home return and the justice
I exacted from Priam's city.
The causes were not spoken aloud,
but the gods heard them
and cast their votes with no opposing voices
into the bloody urn: for Troy's destruction
and the deaths of men.
You can still see the smoke from the city's capture.
The hot blasts of ruin live there yet,

but there is ash, too, dying
as it sends into the air its breaths fattened on rich things.
For all of this we should pay our gods
much-remembering thanks.
We have taken vengeance for insolent robbery.
And for the sake of a woman a city has been leveled
by the biting beast of Argos.
A ravening lion leaped over the wall
and licked its fill of royal blood.
So far my prelude stretches; that is for the gods.
What you've said of your feelings, I've heard and remember.
In very few men is it native
to admire a successful friend without envying him.
For the poison of malice, settling on the heart,
doubles its weight in one who is stricken with envy.
For other matters, we will set up public meetings
and take counsel in full assembly.
What is now well shall remain well; we shall see to it.
But where there is need for healing medicines,
we will try by surgery or cautery
intelligently to avert the disease.
Now I will go in, into my halls, my hearth, my home.
Victory has followed us;
let her be ours still, constantly.

(Enter Clytemnestra.)

Clytemnestra
You citizens, elders of Argos,
I will not be ashamed of speaking to you
of how I love my husband.
With time and familiarity,
modest inhibition dies away.
I will tell of how wretched my life has been
while this man was in Troy—
at first hand I will tell it; it has been *my* life.
First, that a woman should sit in her house,
lonely without her male,

is something terrifying.
She hears so many hateful rumors;
here's one has come, and then another
announcing a greater disaster still,
mouthing the ruin of our house.
If this man here had had as many wounds
as streams of rumor would have it,
he would have had more holes in him than a net.
It was because of these hateful reports
that others have loosened many a cord
as it tightened round my neck.
And that is also why your son
doesn't stand beside me as he should,
the proof of our trust, mine to you, yours to me,
our Orestes.
Do not wonder at this; a loyal ally keeps him safe,
Strophius the Phocian.
He spoke to me of twin troubles:
your danger at Troy, and then that here
the anarchy of the people's voices
might overturn good counsel.
For my own part, the gushing springs of my grief
have dried up;
there's not a drop left.
My eyes are in pain from late watching,
weeping for the beacons that should tell of you,
but never called for firing.
In my dreams, I have started up,
roused by the light strokes of the gnat's flight;
I have seen so much more happen to you
than could be contained within the time
with which I shared my sleep.
But now I have come through all this;
my heart is free of sorrow;
and so I can describe this man of mine—
a watchdog of the house,

the saving forestay of the ship,
the rooted pillar of the towering roof,
the single child of a father,
the land seen by sailors when they had given over hope,
the fairest day to see after the storm,
the springwater stream for the thirsty traveler.
It is sweet indeed to escape the harsh stroke of necessity.
Now, dear heart,
step from the carriage, but do not place on earth, my king,
this foot that trod Troy to destruction.
Servants, to whom I have commanded the task,
let his way lie straight before him strewn with purple,
that justice may guide him to the home he never hoped for.

Agamemnon

Daughter of Leda, guardian of my house,
your speech is a good fit for my absence:
both have stretched out long.
Do not make much of me in this woman's fashion,
nor grovel and gape flatteringly, like some foreigner,
nor strew my path with garments that would make it
an object of ill will;
it is the gods one should honor with such things.
For one who is mortal, for me certainly,
to walk on subtly woven beauties like these
cannot be without fear.
I tell you, honor me as man, not god.
Footmats and embroideries—they sound differently,
they are different. Not to be presumptuous
is the greatest gift the gods can give you.
It's only when a life has ended, and ended well,
that one dare say, "Well done."
I would be cheerful if my life were like this in everything.

Clytemnestra

Then tell me this, and let it be your own true judgment—
Was it through fear of the gods
that you made this vow?

Agamemnon
I said, if any man ever did, what I knew would happen.
Clytemnestra
And what of Priam, if he had conquered as you have?
Agamemnon
He would certainly have trodden on the tapestry.
Clytemnestra
Don't be ashamed, then, of human reproach.
Agamemnon
Yes, but the ill repute of the people's voices
has a great power.
Clytemnestra
He that is not envied is also not admired.
Agamemnon
A woman should not long so for a fight.
Clytemnestra
In those that win, yielding is graceful.
Agamemnon
Do you set such store on victory in this dispute?
Clytemnestra
Let me have my way. You are the victor
if you yield readily.
Agamemnon
Well, if you will—here, someone undo my sandals,
that are like slaves for the treading of my foot.
And as I walk upon these lovely cloths,
I pray against the envious eye of the gods
lest from afar it strike me.
It's a great shame to spoil a house's wealth,
these weavings so dear in price, with the dirt of treading feet.
Enough of this.

(Steps down.)

Bring in this stranger here, and use her kindly.
No one chooses to become a slave.
This woman is the very flower, picked out
from the spoils of war;

as a gift from the army to me, she followed me.
Well, since I've been subdued to listen to you,
I will go into my house, treading on purple.

Clytemnestra

There is a sea—and who shall drain it dry?—
nourishing a spring, always new, an abundance of purple
to be bought with silver for the dyeing of garments.
This house, my lord, has store enough of it,
thanks be to the gods.
This house does not know poverty.
I would have vowed the treading of many garments,
to win the safe return of your life.
Zeus, Zeus, that brings all to perfection,
perfect my prayer.

Chorus

Why this fluttering, insistent terror
that keeps guard before my heart?
Is the song prophetic
that rises unbidden?
Time has grown old since the ships
set out to Troy.
With my eyes I am my own witness
to their homecoming.
But nonetheless, my spirit within me
drones this tune of the Furies,
accompanied by no lyre,
a song taught by none but itself.
But I pray that what I expect may fall away,
a lie, into unfulfillment.
The black blood of a man,
when once it has fallen to the earth in his death,
who shall conjure it back again with any incantation?
If there were no fates appointed by the gods,
my heart would have outstripped my tongue

and poured this out.
But now in the dark it mutters, in heart-anguish.

Clytemnestra
In with you too, now, Cassandra,
since Zeus has made you a sharer
in the sacrifices in our house.
Get down from that carriage;
none of your high spirit of pride.
Chorus
You are taken, a quarry in fate's net;
obey her—
though I will understand if you don't.
Clytemnestra
If she has anything besides her swallow twitterings,
a barbaric speech that no one knows,
I'll try to persuade her within her understanding.
Chorus
Follow her. What she says is the best there is for you;
leave the carriage; obey her.
Clytemnestra
I have no time to waste here with her
outside the palace.
The sheep stand ready for slaughter
in front of the hearth at the center of the house.
(*To Cassandra.*)
You, if you're going to do anything that I tell you,
do it quickly.
(*To Chorus.*)
Don't speak to her any more; use your hands;
that's all these foreigners understand.
Chorus
She looks like a wild thing newly caught.
Clytemnestra
Of course she does; she's come here

not yet knowing how to wear the curb bit,
till she's frothed out her spirit in blood.

(*Exit Clytemnestra.*)

Chorus

Come, you poor girl,
yield to what must be; wear your yoke for the first time.
I pity her.

Cassandra

Oh! Oh! Oh! Oh, the land!
Lord Apollo! Lord Apollo!

Chorus

Why do you raise such dismal cries to Apollo?

Cassandra

Oh! Oh! Oh! Oh, the land!
Lord Apollo! Lord Apollo!

Chorus

Again she calls upon the god.

Cassandra

Lord Apollo! Lord Apollo! God of the streets,
god of destruction! Now again, god of my destruction,
and so easily. Lord Apollo! Lord Apollo!
God of my destruction! God of the streets!
Through what streets have you led me now,
to what house?

Chorus

To that of the sons of Atreus.

Cassandra

Yes, to a house that the gods hate;
it has been witness of so many
murders of kin, butcheries,
bowl full of man's blood, ground soaked in shed blood.
The children, the babies screaming of their cut throats,
of their flesh roasted and eaten by their father.

Chorus

> We have heard of your fame as a prophet;
> but we need no foretellers here.

Cassandra

> Oh, what does she plan?
> It is a great evil against the house
> that she is planning.
> Is this what you bring to consummation?
> You have cleaned him in the bath till his skin shined,
> the husband to share your bed.
> And how shall I tell the consummation?
> It would be quick: the line of clutching hands,
> stretching out, one hooked to another.

Chorus

> I don't understand; what baffles me is the dimness
> of what comes from the gods in words.

Cassandra

> Oh! Oh! Oh!
> A net; a net of death.
> But the meshes are the bedfellow, the accomplice in murder.
> Look at that! Look at that!
> Keep away the bull from the cow!
> She will take him in the folds of the robe
> with the trick of the black horn.
> She strikes! He falls! He falls
> in the water of the bath.
> That is his end, I tell you,
> a treacherous murder in a cauldron.

Chorus

> What good word ever came to mankind from the prophets?
> The wordy tricks of the prophets
> bring terrors for us to understand.

Cassandra

> It is my own suffering on top of his
> that my tongue spills out.

(To the god.)

Where is this you have brought me to in my sorrow?
For nothing but to share his death; what else?
Chorus
　It is for yourself you cry out this tuneless tune.
　Like the brown nightingale, that can never have
　enough of song,
　　as she cries "Itys! Itys!" for her life rich in sorrows,
　and her mind loves pity for herself.
Cassandra
　Oh! The life of the shrill-voiced nightingale!
　The gods covered *her* with a feathered body;
　I tell you, they gave her a *sweet* life,
　and her cries are not cries of sorrow.
　But what remains for me
　is the splitting of the flesh with the two-edged spear.
Chorus
　What is this word you have spoken all too clearly?
　A newborn child could understand.
　The bite of murder has pierced me
　as you whimper at your painful fortune.
　It is a heartbreak to hear you.
Cassandra
　Now my prophecy shall no longer peer from behind veils
　like a newly married bride.
　No, it will rush on, a wind brightly blowing
　into the sun's rising.
　I will not school you in riddles any longer.
　The revelers have drunk, to whet their courage more,
　man's blood, and so they abide in the house,
　and none shall expel them: they are the Furies,
　that attend on the murder of kin.
　The song they sing
　is the song of the primal destruction,
　when the mind is blinded.
　And each of the Furies has spat in disgust
　on the brother's bed that hates its violator.

Am I an archer that missed,
or have I hit the mark?
Make your sworn oath
that I know the story of the ancient sins
of this house.

Chorus
I do wonder at you,
that you, reared beyond the sea and speaking a strange tongue
should talk of these things as if you had been there.
Cassandra
It was Apollo the prophet
that charged me with the gift of prophecy,
Apollo that breathed his grace into me.
Chorus
He fell in love with you?
Did you come to the breeding of children?
Cassandra
I promised the god and cheated him.
Chorus
Had you already got your gift of prophecy?
Cassandra
Oh yes, I used to tell my countrymen all that would happen,
but since my offense against him,
no one believed a word of mine.
Chorus
Ah, but to us right now, you seem to prophesy truly.
Cassandra
Look! Look! You see them! The young ones,
sitting on the house like dream phantoms.
They are the likenesses of those children dead and gone,
killed by those they loved;
their hands are full of meat, their own flesh.
You can see it clearly; they carry the pitiful load
of their guts, and their father has tasted them.
I tell you, there is punishment for this,

and someone is plotting it,
a lion, but a coward, a housekeeper
in the bed of the returning lord—
O mine, my lord.
The captain of the ships, the sacker of Ilium,
he knows not what tongue is licking him,
the tongue of the hateful bitch, her ears pricked,
like a secret blind vengeance.
The woman will murder the man.
It is all one to me, if you do not believe any of this;
what difference?
It is to be and will come.
Soon you will stand here and say of me, in pity,
she was too true a prophet.

Chorus
The feast of Thyestes, and the flesh of the children,
I understand and shudder.
But for the rest I heard from you,
I have fallen off the course and run wide.

Cassandra
I tell you, you will live to see Agamemnon's death.

Chorus
Wretched girl, hold your tongue in piety.

>   (*She starts tearing off her robe and garlands.*)

Cassandra
Why should I have these mockeries about me,
the prophet's garlands round my neck?
Look, Apollo himself undoes his prophetess
of her prophetic mantle.
Enrich some other girl with blinded madness,
some other girl than me.
Yet, all the same, I shall not die dishonored by the gods.
A wanderer outcast will come to take vengeance for me;
he will kill the mother in whom he was seeded,
and will avenge his father,
and put a coping stone of ruin for those he loved.

His father's corpse shall bring him home again.
I will go and face it; I will face my death.
These gates before me here, I call you now by name:
the gates of death.
But I pray that the stroke that reaches me
may be a mortal stroke,
that without struggle, as the blood runs freely,
in easy death I may close these eyes of mine.

Chorus

You are a woman that has suffered much,
and understood much.
But if you truly know your fate,
why do you walk up to the altar steadfastly,
like an ox?

Cassandra

There is no escape, my friends; the time is full.
I pity you, father, and your noble children.

(She recoils.)

Chorus

What is it? What is the fear that turns you back?

(Cassandra shudders.)

Chorus

What made you shudder?
Or is it something in your mind that disgusts you?

Cassandra

The house! It reeks of murder, of dripping blood!

Chorus

What? It's just the blood of sacrificed animals.

Cassandra

No, it is just like the smell of a grave.
Still—I will go into the house,
to mourn with cries my own and Agamemnon's deaths.
I have enough of life.

(Exit Cassandra.)

Chorus

Here is this king, to whom the blessed gods granted
the sacking of Priam's city;
he came home with all the honors that the gods gave him.
But now, if he shall pay for the blood of the past—

Agamemnon (from within)

I've been hit! I am hurt to death.

Chorus

Hush! Who is it that cries out, hurt to death?

Agamemnon

I'm hit again!

Chorus

It is the king crying out; I think all is over.
But let us plan safety for ourselves—if we can.
1. My vote is to cry, Help! to the citizens
to come to the palace.
2. Yes, and at once, I think,
to catch them red-handed with dripping sword.
3. At least we should do something.
It isn't the moment for hesitation.
4. But we can see. This is a kind of first act;
it looks like the beginning of a tyranny.
5. Yes, it does—because we're wasting time.
Their hands don't sleep.
6. I do not know what would be best.
7. One cannot by talking bring the dead to life again.
8. Are we then, in order to stretch our own lives,
to yield to a government that shames our royal house?
9. No. Death is better than that.
Death is better than subjection to a tyranny.

(Enter Clytemnestra.)

Clytemnestra

This was my day of trial; I have thought of it
enough and long enough, a trial of an old quarrel
years and years old.

He is dead, and the sequence ended.
This is how I managed that he should not escape,
nor defend himself from death.
I threw about him an encompassing net,
as it might be for fish, all-entangling,
an evil wealth of cloak.
I struck him twice. He gave two groans,
and his body went limp;
as he lay there, I gave him a third,
in honor of that god that keeps the dead
securely in the underworld.
This was my grace and prayer for him.
So, as he lay there, he gasped out his spirit,
choking, poured out a sharp stream of blood
and struck me with the dark bloody shower.
I rejoiced as much as the new-sown earth
rejoices in the glad rain of Zeus,
when the buds strike in earth's womb.
So it is, you old men of Argos here;
be glad, if you can. I triumph in it.

Chorus

I wonder at your tongue,
that you should boast like this over a dead husband.

Clytemnestra

You try me out as if I were a woman that cannot think.
But my heart doesn't tremble.
Here is Agamemnon, my husband, now a corpse—
his deadness the work of this right hand of mine,
an efficient craftsman.
That is how *that* is.

Chorus

Woman, what evil thing have you eaten
that grows in the earth,
what draught have you tasted that comes from the salt sea,
that you have taken upon you so horrible a sacrifice
and the curse of the people's voice?

You have cast away, you have torn apart,
and you shall be cast and torn away from the city,
a monstrous object of hate to the citizens.

Clytemnestra
Now it's against me that you proclaim banishment,
but in the old days you brought nothing against that man,
who, with all the indifference of one whose pastures are full
of teeming flocks, rich in wool,
had no care for the death of a lamb.
He sacrificed his own daughter,
dearest pain of my womb,
to charm the contrariness of Thracian winds.
For this, should you not have banished him,
payment for his polluting wickedness?
No, you are a careful hearer and harsh judge
only of *my* acts.
Threaten away! I tell you now, if once you conquer me
in a fair fight, I'll be your subject;
but if God gives another outcome,
you will get an education in discretion
and learn it thoroughly, though the knowledge
comes very late.

Chorus
You think big thoughts, and you scream proud defiance,
as though the bloody smear of your success
had maddened your mind.
The smear of blood—I can see it in your eyes.
But still you must pay stroke for stroke,
with no friend to take your part.

Clytemnestra
By the justice due to my child,
by the Fury, in whose honor I cut this man's throat,
my hope treads not within the hall of Fear
so long as Aegisthus lights the hearth fire for me,

my loyal friend, as he has always been,
shield for my daring.
There lies Agamemnon, this girl's seducer—
he was the darling of all the women of Troy—
and there she is, our prophet,
that shared his bed, a faithful whore
that spoke her auguries for him.
Both have suffered as they deserved.
He died as I said, and she has sung her swan song in death,
and lies with him, her lover.
But to me she brought an additional side dish
to *my* pleasure in bed.

Chorus
    O my king, my king,
    how shall I sorrow for you?
    Who shall bury him? Who shall keen him?
    Will you dare to do this, to make lament for him,
    you who killed him, your husband?
Clytemnestra
    The care of that concerns you not at all.
    It is by our hand that he fell, that he died,
    and we shall bury him
    with no cries of mourning from this house.
    But his daughter Iphigeneia, as is right,
    will welcome her father by the River of Sorrows
    and throw her arms around him and kiss him.
Chorus
    This is but the exchange of insult for insult.
    The pirate plunders the pirate,
    the killer pays for the killing.
Clytemnestra
    For my part, I am willing to make a sworn compact
    with the evil spirit of this house
    to be satisfied with things as they are.
    I will be utterly content with a small part of wealth,

if I can banish from these halls
the madness of mutual bloodletting.

(*Enter Aegisthus.*)

Aegisthus

O happy light, day of justified revenge!
Now I will say that the gods
in watchfulness so high above the earth
still bear an eye on the sorrows of mortals to avenge them.
Now I take pleasure to have seen this man
lying here in the robes that were
the nets of the Furies for him,
paying for the plots his father's hand contrived.
This is the plain story.
Atreus was this man's father,
and his brother Thyestes was my father.
Both were Pelops's sons;
The two of them were in dispute about the throne,
and Atreus banished my father from city and home.
The unlucky Thyestes later returned.
But the vile Atreus, father of the dead man here,
gave my father a banquet of welcome.
He pretended to celebrate a day of feasting
on flesh slaughtered for meat,
in all hospitality,
but the meat he gave my father was his own children's.
The feet and the ends of the fingers he put apart and hid,
So Thyestes in ignorance ate the other parts,
a meal that brought a curse, as you see, on all the race.
Later, when he discovered what awful act he had committed,
he moaned aloud, recoiled, and vomited up the bloody mess.
"A doom intolerable will overtake," he said,
"the house of Pelops. So perish every one of all your breed."
That is why you can see this man fallen dead here,
and I am justly the one who stitched together his murder.
I am the remaining son, and while I was still
in swaddling clothes

he drove me out along with my luckless father.
But when I grew to manhood, justice brought me back.
Mine was the whole contriving of the evil plot.
So glorious the result, that now I would welcome death itself,
having seen him in the traps of justice.

Chorus

Aegisthus, I do not respect insolence
at the moment of calamity.
Do you say that with aforethought you killed Agamemnon,
that you alone planned this miserable murder?
In that case, I do not think your life will escape
the justice of the public curse, the stoning.

Aegisthus

Do you talk back to me, you who sit at the lower oar,
when we are in possession of the upper deck?
You will find out, despite your age,
how uncomfortable such learning is for an old man,
when discretion is the lesson set.
Chains in old age and hunger's pangs
are the very sharpest healing prophets of the mind.
Don't you see this when you see?

Chorus

Why didn't you kill him yourself, with your cowardly soul?
No, your partner, the woman, did the killing,
to be the pollution of the land and
the curse of the gods.
But I tell you, Orestes still sees the light of day,
that he may come home, and with good luck on his side
be conquerer and the death of both of you.

Aegisthus

Since you're resolved to act and talk like this,
you'll soon know—
here, my bodyguards, this is your work, right here.

Clytemnestra

No, dearest, no. Let us do no further evils.

Those that there are, are many, a bloody harvest;
we have a good store of calamity.
No, no bloodletting.
Good old men, off with you to your houses.
Yield to what must be, before you suffer.
What we did had to be done.

Aegisthus

No, but to have them letting their tongues
blossom in insolence, to throw their empty threats about—
You lack all brains, so to abuse your master.

Chorus

It does not fit an Argive to fawn on a villain.

Aegisthus

I will get even with you in the days to come.

Chorus

Not if the Spirit brings Orestes home.

Aegisthus

I know the diet of exiles is rich in hope.

Chorus

Yes, do things, grow fat, pollute justice—while you can.

Aegisthus

You know you will pay me for your foolishness.

Chorus

Boast, do; be bold—a cock beside your hen.

Clytemnestra

Do not pay heed to their vain yappings. I
and you together will make all things well,
for we are masters of this house.

THE LIBATION BEARERS

(*Enter Orestes and Pylades.*)

Orestes

Hermes, god of the underworld,
Hermes, protector of my father's sovereign rights,
be now my savior, my ally, as I supplicate you.
For I come to this land a returned exile,
and here upon this mound, my father's grave,
I call on him to give ear to me and hear.
I dedicate a lock of my hair for mourning.
For, father, I wasn't there to raise my voice
in sorrow at your death.

(*Enter Electra and Chorus.*)

What is this I see?
What is this band of women
all in black? What can have happened?
For I see my sister Electra coming,
in deep mourning as she would be.
O Zeus, grant that I may avenge my father!
Be my ally.

Electra

Ladies in waiting that tend my house,
give me your counsel.
What am I to say as I pour the libation of mourning?
How can I speak with good will, how pray to my father?
Can I say, coming from *my* mother,
"A gift from a loving wife to loving husband"?
I haven't the audacity for that.
I cannot tell what I should say,
as I pour the oils on my father's grave.
My friends, be my partners in counsel.
For ours is a common grief for the house;
do not through fear of anyone
hide your thoughts in your heart.
Speak, if you've anything to say.

Chorus
　　I will speak then, since you bid me,
　　for this grave of your father I revere like an altar,
　　and my words will be what's in my mind.
Electra
　　Speak.
Chorus
　　Pour the holy oils, and say:
　　"For those that are his well-wishers—"
Electra
　　Whom shall I address as that?
Chorus
　　First yourself, and then whoever hates Aegisthus.
Electra
　　So my prayer will be for me and for you?
Chorus
　　Speak it immediately.
Electra
　　Whom shall I add besides?
Chorus
　　Remember Orestes, even if he is not here.
Electra
　　Good, good! How well you do instruct me.
Chorus
　　Then remember—"On those guilty of the murder—"
Electra
　　What shall I say? I don't know. Tell me.
Chorus
　　Pray that on them there come a god or a man—
Electra
　　As judge or as avenger?
Chorus
　　Say simply, "Who will kill to answer killing?"
Electra
　　Can I with piety ask the gods for that?

Chorus
   Yes, giving evil for evil to an enemy.

Electra
   Hermes of the underworld,
   summon the spirits under earth, who keep their watch
   over my father's house, to hear my prayer.
   And Earth herself, that brings all things to birth,
   and having raised them takes again from them
   the fruit of their fertility—
   here I, that pour to the dead this oil,
   call to my father: Father, have pity on me.
   Kindle dear Orestes to be a light to the house.
   For as it is, both of us are exiles,
   sold by our mother, who has traded us for her man,
   Aegisthus, her partner in our father's murder.
   I pray you that Orestes may come here
   with luck to back him.
   O my father, hear me.
   Grant that I may be more chaste than my mother,
   and have a hand more reverent than hers.
   So far, my prayers for us; but upon our enemies
   I pray, my father, that you come avenging
   and bring a death with justice on the killers.

Chorus
   Drop the streaming tear for a death,
   for dead is our lord;
   drop the tear as a shield,
   for dead is our lord.
   Hear me, lord whom I revere,
   hear me in the infirmity of my mind.
   Let one come to redeem the house,
   a man strong with spear,
   a man strong with sword,
   for dead is our lord.

Electra

  My father has the oils;
  the earth has drunk them.

                          (She sees the lock of Orestes' hair.)

Chorus

  What is it? My heart is dancing with fear.

Electra

  I see on the grave a lock of newly cut hair.

Chorus

  From what man's head, or what girl's?

Electra

  No one but myself could have cut off this hair.

Chorus

  True, those who should mourn him so
  are all his enemies.

Electra

  Yet certainly it looks very like—

Chorus

  Like whose hair? Tell us what you see in it.

Electra

  Certainly it much *resembles* mine.

Chorus

  Could it be a secret gift from him, Orestes?
  How could he have dared to come here?

Electra

  He *sent* it—this hair,
  a mourning tribute to his father.

Chorus

  We have as much occasion to cry as ever,
  if his foot shall never touch this land again.

Electra

  But how can I say without a doubt
  that this precious thing must belong to Orestes—
  dearest to me in all the world?
  Surely hope begins to flatter me.
  Oh, if only the hair could take a human voice

and play the messenger.
Look, look! Here is some more evidence—
footprints, and they are also like mine.
Here are two pairs of tracks
outlined—his, and some other traveler's with him.
The imprint of the heels and the arches
measures exactly with mine.

(*Orestes enters.*)

Orestes
Pray for the rest, that it may turn out well,
acknowledging the prayers that are fulfilled.
Electra
As of now, what have I got with the help of the gods?
Orestes
You have come in sight of
what you long have prayed for.
Electra
Do you know whom I have called upon?
Orestes
I know that you dearly love Orestes.
Electra
And how does that mean my prayers are answered?
Orestes
I am he. Do not look for any man more loved than me.
Electra
Is this some trick, sir, that you are playing upon me?
Orestes
If so, it is a trick upon myself.
Electra
You want to make a mockery of my sorrows.
Orestes
If I mock your sorrows, I would mock my own.
Electra
Can I be talking to you, the real Orestes?
Orestes
You see me in person, and don't know me.

But you saw the mourning lock of hair,
you trod in my footprints, tracking me out,
and then you were ecstatic, you were sure you saw me.
Look, put the lock of cut hair next to your own.
It is a match.
Look at this piece of woven cloth, your handiwork,
your shuttle struck it on the loom;
the beasts are your embroidered pictures.
Do not let joy quite overcome your wits.
For those who should be dearest
hate us both.

Electra

O dearest darling of your father's house,
the tearful hope of the saving seed,
trust in your strength and you will still
win back that house.
O delightful face that has
all four shares of my love:
I must call you father, and to you belongs
the love due to a mother, too—
I hate her, quite justly—
and to you belongs, as well,
the love for my sister, ruthlessly sacrificed;
and you are my brother, trusted and honored
as no one else. May Victory, Justice,
and Zeus, making the third, greatest of all,
be your helpers.

All

May Victory, Justice,
and Zeus, making the third, greatest of all,
be your helpers.

Orestes

Zeus, Zeus, look down and save us!
Behold the brood who have lost their eagle father,
killed in the folds and coils of the deadly viper.
We are orphaned nestlings, and the hunger pinches;

we are not yet fit to bring home what our fathers hunted.
So I and you, dear Electra, can be seen here—
a family without a father—
both sharers of the same exile at home.

Chorus

Zeus, save us!

Electra

Save us! You will lift this house to greatness!

Chorus

Children, saviors of your father's hearth,
silence, lest someone hear you, children,
and bring the news
to the masters of the house—Oh, to see *them*
dead in a fiery ooze of pitch!

Orestes

The strong oracle of Apollo will not let me down,
that oracle that bade me run this risk.
He spoke of many things in his warning voice,
of chill destruction under the warm heart,
if I should fail to pursue my father's murderers.
"Kill them," he said, "to match their killings."
Otherwise, he said, with my own life
I myself would pay, with a multitude of dreadful sufferings
—with the anger of evil spirits
from under the earth, malignant against mortals,
diseases on us both, that would climb on our flesh
with savage jaws, cankers that eat into our bodies' nature,
and a white down on top of the sick parts.
Of all assaults of the Furies he spoke,
that my father's blood would bring to bear upon me
as I gaze clearly into the darkness, with eyebrows active.
For the arrow of those below, that flies in darkness,
and madness, and empty terrors waking at night,
drive, haunt, and chase from the city the tortured body.
The unseen anger of the father bars his son from the altars.

And at the last, unhonored and unloved,
in utter ruin, wasted to dryness, death.
Should I not believe the truth of oracles like these?
Even if I didn't believe, the deed must be done.
For there are many desires converging in one,
the gods' commands, my great grief for my father—
the thought that those who devastated Troy
shall become subjects of two women.
His (i.e., Aegisthus's) spirit is womanish. If it is not,
he will soon know what he is.
Chorus
O great fates, bring all to fulfillment
through Zeus in the way that the path of justice is.
Let enemy tongue pay for enemy tongue;
for bloody stroke, let a bloody stroke be paid.
"He who acts shall suffer"—
this is the voice of the story grown old in time.
Orestes
Father, father most dread,
what shall I say or do
to bring you here from your far land
where the bed of the grave holds you,
where darkness is your share of the light?
Chorus
Child, the due mourning of fathers and parents
shall set the hunt on.
Electra
Hear, O my father, in turn,
my grief and my tears.
Hear the twin dirge of your children by the graveside.
The grave has welcomed us,
as suppliant and exile, both alike.
Chorus
If the god so wills,
he may bring to pass more tuneful songs,
and instead of dirges at the grave

a hymn of welcome shall greet
the loving cup in the royal palace.

Orestes

Would that under Troy's walls, father,
you had been cut down by the spear of some Lycian soldier.
Then you would have left in your house
a fair fame, and established for your children
a life for all to admire.

Electra

Yes, father, would that beneath Troy's walls
you had died. I had rather those who killed you
should have died as you died.

Chorus

In that, my child, you speak of something
greater than gold, a great chance
and a greater bliss.
Certainly you can *speak* of it,
but there comes the sound of the stroke
of the double lash.
The champions of the one side are even now under the earth,
and the hands of the masters of the house are unholy—
those hateful creatures—
and grow more so against the children.

Orestes

Zeus, O Zeus, send up to us from the world below
revenge, revenge on the violent sacrilegious hand.

Chorus

May it be mine to sing a strong cry of triumph
over a man striken and a woman dying.

Electra

When will the hand of Zeus strike with power?
When will he split the head?
Let it come in such form as the land can believe.
After the days of injustice I demand justice.

Chorus

It is the law that the drops of blood

fallen on the ground demand more blood.
The plague of the Furies calls aloud
on behalf of those already dead
for another destruction to crown the first.

Orestes

Alas, Earth, sovereignties of the underworld,
you all-mastering curses of the dead,
look upon us, look upon the remnants
of the stock of Atreus, so perplexed.
Look upon the dishonor of the house.
Whom shall one turn to?

Chorus

My loving heart is shaken again
when I hear this pitiable cry;
my hope fails me; my heart grows blacker
as I listen.

Electra

Mother, all-daring, you were his enemy,
and you dared to give him an enemy's funeral;
without citizens for the carrying forth of their king,
without dirge you buried him, unmourned.

Orestes

But she shall pay for the dishonoring of my father,
by favor of the gods, by favor of these hands of mine.
When I have cut my foes away from life,
may my death come upon me.

Chorus

She cut off his hands to stuff in his armpits,
let me tell you; she did that,
she who buried him as you say,
seeking to render his death something
unbearable to you his children.

Electra

I was shut up
in a corner of the house, like a vicious dog.
I found a stream of tears readier than laughter;

I poured out my tears in flood in secret.
Hear this, my father, and write it
in the tablets of your mind.

Chorus

Drive the word through the ears
to the steadying pace of the mind.

Orestes

I bid you, father, come to us—
we love you.

Electra

I have given you my tears;
I invite you.
O gods, grant just fulfillment!

Orestes

Father, killed in ways unroyal,
give me control of the house that was yours!

Electra

Father, I, too, need this from you—
to destroy Aegisthus and to escape.

Orestes

War god will clash with war god.

Electra

Justice with Justice.

Orestes

O Earth, send up my father to oversee the fight!

Electra

Grant us victory!

Orestes

Remember the bath in which you died.

Electra

Remember the robes, put to new use as a net.

Orestes

Will these taunts rouse you from your sleep, my father?

Electra

Will you lift up your beloved head?

Orestes

Send us Justice!

Grant us a handhold to match *their* hands.

Electra

Hear this last cry of all, my father:

Have pity on your brood here upon your grave.

Orestes

Do not blot out this seed of Pelops's children.

For if they live you are not dead, in death.

Children are voices of salvation to a dead man;

they are like corks that keep the nets afloat.

Electra

Hear us

Electra and Orestes

and come to the light.

Chorus

Enough. Now go, since you are rightly set on action.

Orestes

We will, but it is not amiss to know

why she has sent these offerings, what story moved her

to pay for an inexpiable crime

so many years after.

Chorus

That godless woman

was driven by dreams and by night-wandering terrors

to send these offerings.

She thought that she gave birth to a snake—

that is how she told it.

Orestes

How did her story end?

Chorus

She wrapped the snake in swaddling clothes,

like a baby.

Orestes

What food did it need?

Chorus
She gave it the breast, in her dream.
Orestes
How did the hateful thing not hurt the nipple?
Chorus
It did. It drew clots of blood with the milk.
Orestes
It is a vision of a man.
Chorus
And after that, she sent these funeral offerings;
she hoped that they would cure all that was wrong.
Orestes
This is *my* prayer, by this land, by my father's grave:
may this dream find fulfillment for me!
For if the snake came from the same place *I* did,
and sucked the breast that gave me sustenance,
mixed the dear milk
with clots of blood, and she was terrified
at what had happened—then, it must be so that,
as she raised this fearful monster,
she must die violently!
For I that became that very snake will kill her,
even as the dream has said.
Chorus
So may it turn out! For the rest,
instruct us that are your friends.
Orestes
My sister must go inside—
hide this plan we have arranged—
that those who killed with treachery a prince
may themselves be caught with treachery and die
in the same snare—as our lord, Apollo, has prophesied.
I will disguise myself as a foreigner,
and come with Pylades here to the courtyard gates.
And if once I cross the threshold,
if once I find him upon my father's throne,

or if he comes to speak to me, face to face,
before he says, "Where is this foreigner from?"
with my quick blade I will send him to his death.
The Fury unstinted of murder will now drink
a third draught of blood full strength.
Do you, Electra, keep careful watch in the house,
and you, my friends, keep
a very heedful hold upon your tongue.
The rest, Pylades here must oversee,
who has guided my sword to success in other contests.

(*Exeunt Orestes, Pylades, Electra.*)

Chorus

Many indeed are the terrors
the earth breeds, causes for fear;
and the bosom of the deep teems
with monsters repulsive;
overhead hang the lights
that menace in midair;
and all creatures, winged and earthbound,
can tell of the wrath of the wind-driven hurricane.
But who shall tell the tale
of man's overbold spirit?
And who can tell how far those passionate loves
can dare?
The love passion of the woman, winning victory,
unloving, perverts the gentle mating
of beasts and men alike.
What of *this* vile marriage tie
accursed by the house, what of the designs
that the woman crafted against her soldier-husband?
Deep-rooted is the trunk of Justice's tree,
and fate forges her sword on her behalf,
and to the house the glorious Fury
brings a child at long last to exact
penalty for the pollution of old bloodshed.

(*Enter Orestes and Pylades.*)

Orestes

Hello, within there! Do you hear me knocking?
Who is there? Who is at home?

Servant

I hear you.

Orestes

For the last time, come out,
if this house of Aegisthus has any hospitality.

(Enter servant.)

Servant

What is your country? What is your need?

Orestes

Take a message to your masters,
to whom I come. I have news for them.
Hurry, for night's car hastens on to dark,
and it is time for travelers to cast anchor
at some house where strangers are welcomed.

(Exit servant; enter Clytemnestra.)

Clytemnestra

Sirs, say what you have to say.
You shall have all that fits this house to give—
warm baths, and comfortable beds,
and properly respectful faces to tend you.

Orestes

I am Daulieus, a Phocian, a stranger to you.
I was going to Argos, on my private business,
and a men met me as I journeyed,
a man unknown to me before—and asked me about the road
(his name was Strophius, also a Phocian):
"If, sir, you are going to Argos in any case,
would you remember, truly, to tell Orestes' parents
'Orestes is dead'—please
do not forget this message. For now the ribs
of the brazen urn hide the dust of this man much mourned."

Clytemnestra

Ah! Your story tells our utter ruin.

Curse of this house, how tough a wrestler
you are against us!
You have stripped me of those I loved;
and now Orestes—
he had been wise, he had been taken away
and kept his foot out of destruction's mud.
He was one hope.

Orestes

I would I could have
made the acquaintance of such noble hosts
through happy events.
But I had promised and pledged my word.

Clytemnestra

You will be treated with just as much dignity,
you will be just as good a friend to the house.
If you had not, another would have come and given the news.
Bring this man to the men's guest chambers.
We ourselves will give your message to
the master of the house.

(Exeunt all but Chorus.)

Chorus

When shall we show
the strength of our voices for Orestes?
O sacred land, where our king lies, that led the fleet,
now hear our words, now come to our help;
now is the time for Hermes of the Underworld
to watch, to preside
over our deadly conflicts of the sword.

(Enter nurse.)

But here I sees Orestes' nurse in tears.
Where are you going, Cilissa?

Nurse

The mistress bade me call Aegisthus speedily
to meet these strangers, that as man to man
he may come and understand this news of theirs.
To the servants she shows a solemn face of sorrow,

but behind the eyes there is a lurking smile
in honor of events that have turned out well—
for her—but for the house a sheer disaster.
He surely too will hear and will rejoice
when he has grasped the story. Ah me! Ah me!
So much has happened in the past to the house
that was hard to bear—a mingled draught of sorrow
that made my heart in my breast an agony.
But never did I endure the like of this;
all the rest of the cup I have drained with patience,
but my Orestes, my life's work,
whom I took from his mother's hand and raised him up!
My nights broken with his crying, all the many
tasks so uselessly performed—I bore them all;
for a baby is so helpless; you must tend him like an animal,
the nurse's mind instead of his own; swaddled,
it does not say what ails it—hunger or thirst
or a wet diaper—the child's young belly
is autonomous! I was the prophet
of his needs, but often deceived, you may be sure,
and so the laundress that made all white again;
a nurse is often nurse and cleaner both,
and *I* doubled in both trades, as I took Orestes
to raise as his father's heir. And now I hear
he is dead—O my God!
And I go to fetch this man, this very infection
of our house. He will be glad to hear the news.
Chorus
   You say she bade him come to her. But how?
Nurse
   What do you mean by "how"? I don't understand.
Chorus
   Was he to come with his retinue or on his own?
Nurse
   She bade him bring his personal guards with him.

Chorus

  Tell our cursed master nothing of the sort;
  tell him to come by himself, without a fear,
  and listen; tell him to come quickly, gladly.

Nurse

  Are you a friend to this our present news?

Chorus

  Yes, but what if Zeus means to change
  our present ill weather?

Nurse

  How can that be? The house's hope, Orestes, is gone.

Chorus

  Not yet.

Nurse

  What! Do you have news different from what is said?

Chorus

  Go, give your message; do what your mistress told you.

Nurse

  I will obey your words and go.
  May all be for the best, as the gods will give it!

                                (Exit nurse.)

Chorus

  All I have spoken is justice.
  O Zeus, protect us.
  Make our champion winner over his enemies
  within the house.
  Grant the crowning of the house of the hero;
  grant that he may see the radiant light of freedom
  as it comes out of the veil of dark mist.
  You temperate gods that haunt
  the recesses of the house,
  let no murder of long ago
  breed another sequence.
  Do you, when the share of action comes,
  in answer to her cry of "Child!"

cry, "Father!" and bring to pass
a destruction none can blame.

(*Enter Aegisthus.*)

Aegisthus

I was summoned; my wife's message
brought me here. I learn that there is news
which some strangers have brought,
very unpleasant news—the death of Orestes.
It will be another bloody grief laid for the house to bear,
a house already bitten by an old wound.
What can you tell me of this that is clear to the mind?

Chorus

Go into the house,
and make your own inquiry of the strangers.

Aegisthus

I am very anxious
to see and test the messenger thoroughly—
whether he was present, beside the man as he died,
or only said what he knew from a dim rumor.
I am wide awake; I will not be easily cheated.

(*Exit Aegisthus.*)

Chorus

Zeus, Zeus, what shall I say, from where begin
with prayers and invocations?
How can I find words to express
the loyalty I feel for Orestes?
For now the befouled points
of knives that butcher men
will either achieve the eternal ruin
of Agamemnon's house,
or there shall be one that kindles
the fire and light in freedom's honor,
and will rule throughout the city;
he shall have the great wealth of his fathers.
It shall be Orestes, the beloved of God,
Orestes.

Aegisthus (offstage)
  Oh! Oh!
Chorus
  O my God!

(Enter servant.)

Servant
  O sorrow, sorrow! Our master is killed.
  Sorrow again, Aegisthus is no more.
  Open the doors! It is the deaf I speak to; surely they sleep.
  Open the doors! Where is Clytemnestra?
  What is she doing?
  It seems that now *her* neck is on the block
  to fall, as she has deserved it should.

(Enter Clytemnestra.)

Clytemnestra
  What is this? What does your shouting mean?
Servant
  It is the dead killing the living.
Clytemnestra
  I understand the truth of your riddle.
  We killed by cunning; now we die by cunning.

(Enter Orestes and Pylades.)

Orestes
  Yes, it is *you* I seek. *He* has had enough.
Clytemnestra
  My God, he is dead—dearest, strongest Aegisthus.
Orestes
  You love him, do you? In the same grave you'll lie
  along with him.
Clytemnestra
  Stop, my child. Have some reverence for this breast
  which often, sleeping, you milked to your good,
  squeezing it with your gums.
Orestes
  O Pylades, what shall I do?
  I cannot kill my mother.

Pylades
Where then will be Apollo's prophecies?
Have everyone as enemy rather than the gods.
Orestes (to Clytemnestra)
I mean to kill you beside him.
You rated him in life above my father;
now in death sleep with him. Between the two men,
you love and hate the wrong ones.
Clytemnestra
I raised you and would grow old with you.
Orestes
You killed my father. Would you live with his son?
Clytemnestra
Fate, my child, was a partner in all this.
Orestes
And fate it is that brings this death on you.
Clytemnestra
Do you not fear your mother's curses, child?
Orestes
You brought me to birth, and sold me shamelessly.
Clytemnestra
What was the price I got for you?
Orestes
I am ashamed to insult you openly with *that*.
Clytemnestra
Then you must speak equally of *his* lechery.
It is hard for a woman to live without a man.
I see, my child, you mean to kill your mother.
Orestes
It is you who kill yourself, not I who kill you.
Clytemnestra
Watch out; guard yourself against
your mother's furious hounds.
Orestes
If I let you go, shall I not fear
my father's furious hounds?

Clytemnestra
I think I am singing my dirge at the grave's edge,
and that is vain.
This is the snake I brought to birth and suckled.
Orestes
The fear in your dream was a true prophet; yes.
You violated in killing; you are violated in suffering.
                    (*Exeunt Orestes, Clytemnestra, Pylades.*)
Chorus
Justice has come at last.
Justice has come, with its heavy revenge.
Orestes, by Apollo's word,
has obtained all his destined lot;
he yielded so prudently
to what the god told him to do.
The might of the gods is always master
in action against the wicked.
Arise, O house! For far too long a time
you have lain level with the earth.
Soon time that brings all to accomplishment
shall cross the threshold of this palace,
and we shall cry aloud,
"The strangers have fallen! They have vanished
from the palace they tenanted!"
There is light for us to see.
                    (*Enter Orestes and Pylades, with the bodies.*)
Orestes
See there, the two princes of this land.
They killed my father, plundered the house.
They were solemn as they sat on their thrones.
They are dear friends to one another still—
                    (*He points at the two bodies.*)
so at least you would think from how they are now.
And look you, now (*he holds up an imaginary robe*)
look at the traps for my poor father,
the tyings of his feet,

the fetters of his hands: this was the covering of the man.
Let the father see it—not my father, of course,
but the father that looks down upon
all that is done here, the Sun-Father.
This robe is my witness
that the sword of Aegisthus stained it.
Time has deepened the stain of murdered blood
that, joining in, has spoiled
the many other dyes in the embroidery.
I praise my father; now I am here to lament him.
You I address, you woven cloth that murdered
my father. Yes, I have pain
for the deed, for the suffering, for our whole race.
I have the pollution, the undesirable
fruits of my victory.

Chorus

Ah me for this present trouble—
and now there is another.

Orestes

I want you to know—for how it will end I don't know—
it is as if I were driving
a team of horses clear out of the course.
They are bolting with me, they have the better of me!
There is fear in my heart that is ready to sing;
I have a dance there under my anger.
Yes, I confess
I killed my mother, and I did so justly.
I cite as the chief cure for this awful thing I did—
Apollo and his prophecies.
He spoke to me and said: "If you do this,
you shall be clear of evil blame."
I will go to Apollo's shrine,
his seat at the navel of the earth.
In days to come I charge all Argives keep
within their memory how these evils happened.

Chorus

But what you did was right! Do not blame yourself.
You gave its freedom to all the city of Argos;
you neatly cut off the heads of the two dragons.

Orestes

Oh! Oh!
Can these be women? Look! They are like Gorgons.
Their robes are dark, and they themselves a mass
of writhing snakes!

Chorus

What are these visions that torment you?

Orestes

These are not *visions;*
they are clearly what they are—
my mother's furious hounds.

Chorus

It is the fresh blood on your hand that does it.
Apollo with a touch
shall make you free of these torments.

Orestes

You don't see them; but *I* do.
I am driven. I cannot stay.

(Exit Orestes.)

Chorus

May the god look on you
with kindly aspect, guarding you throughout
the perils you must meet!
In the beginning was the child-eating
and the sufferings of Thyestes.
Then came the murder of the king,
cut down in his bath.
And now? Is it a rescuer,
or must I call him a destruction?
When will it find completion? When will it end?
When will the fierceness of our ruin
fall again to its sleep?

THE EUMENIDES

(*Enter Orestes and Apollo.*)

Orestes
  O King Apollo, you know not to be unjust.
Apollo
  I will not desert you; to the end your guardian,
  beside you and afar, I shall prove myself
  not gentle to your enemies.
  Now you see these crazed creatures,
  sunk in sleep, its prisoners,
  these ancient children;
  nor god nor man nor beast will touch them.
  Their birth, too, was for evil, for evil darkness
  is where they live.
  I will protect you; but you must flee from them.
  For they will hunt you
  through all the length of the earth, as you stride onward,
  over the ground worn by your feet,
  over the seas, and then, over the island cities.
  This task of yours will herd you on—do not weary
  before it ends; go to the city of Pallas Athena;
  there clasp your arms around the ancient image,
  and sit. In that place we will find judges,
  and speeches as our engine to enchant them;
  so you shall be freed entirely from your troubles.
  I *did* persuade you to kill your mother.
  Remember that; do not let fear conquer your mind.
  Now, Hermes, my blood-brother,
  guard him and be to him
  a very escort, a protection;
  be his shepherd, for he is my suppliant.
                    (*Exeunt Orestes and Apollo; enter Clytemnestra.*)

Clytemnestra's Ghost
    You sleep! Aha! What need have I of sleepers?
    Because of you I am dishonored among
    the other dead; those dead that I have killed
    never let up their abuses against me.
    I wander, shamed, among the perished people.
    I tell you, I have the greatest blame among them,
    I that have suffered such outrages from those
    dearest to me,
    and no god shows his anger on my behalf,
    though I was slaughtered by hands that killed their mother.
    Look here, look at that wound upon my heart.
    For when the mind is asleep, its eyes are bright;
    by day men have less vision of what is destined.
    You have licked up many of my offerings,
    ritual feasts at dead of night,
    shared with no other god.
    Now I see all of this trodden underfoot,
    neglected. He has slipped away, like a fawn,
    lightly—even from the closest drawn of nets.
    Hear how I plead for my very soul!
    Take heed, you goddesses beneath the earth.
    For it is I that call you, in a dream,
    Clytemnestra.
    The man has escaped!
    Follow him, follow him, waste him.

                                    (*Exit Clytemnestra.*)

Chorus
    We have suffered—and in vain!
    Evil beyond enduring!
    He slipped from the net; I lost my prey.
    Apollo, what a thief you are.
    You are young and have ridden down
    the ancient gods. You stole away a mother-murderer.
    Apollo, what a thief you are.
    You are young and have ridden down

the ancient gods. You stole away a mother-murderer.
This is what the new gods do,
seat dripping blood, hand and foot.
You see the earth's navel in blood,
a massive curse.
Apollo shall have my bitterness;
Orestes shall not be free.

Apollo

Out with you! And be quick!
Go, rid the prophetic sanctuary of your presence,
lest the winged gleaming snake,
sped by the golden bowstring, overtake you!
Then in your agony you will vomit
black foam from your lungs; you will spew out
those lumps of congealed blood you have drawn in.
It is not fit your feet should touch my house here.
You belong where sentences of execution
are carried out, the gouging of eyes,
cutting of throats, castration of young boys,
mutilation, stoning; where the whimperings
of men impaled cry pity. Be gone!

Chorus

Apollo, culprit!

Apollo

How so? Talk long enough to tell me that, no more!

Chorus

You gave an oracle that the stranger should kill his mother.

Apollo

I gave an oracle that he should
avenge his father.

Chorus

And so you promised to accept new blood.

Apollo

And I have bade him to approach this house.

Chorus

—insulting us, who dogged him here.

Apollo
You are not fit to approach a shrine like this.
Chorus
This is our appointed task.
Apollo
What is this fine appointed task that you boast of?
Chorus
Drive from their houses those that kill their mothers.
Apollo
What of the woman who has killed her man?
Chorus
She is not of blood kin, not of blood kin.
Apollo
In your argument, the bond of marriage
is discounted utterly—yet from Aphrodite
the very dearest things come to human kind;
for man and woman, the bed, when justly kept,
is greater than any oath that can be sworn.
The goddess Athena shall oversee this trial.
Chorus
I am drawn by blood, mother's blood.
I will seek penalty.
I will hunt out this man.
Apollo
I will protect this man.

(*The scene changes to Athens and Athena's temple.*)
Orestes
Lady Athena, by the command of Apollo
I come; receive me kindly, though I am guilty.
I have crossed over dry land and over sea,
and so I approach your house and image, goddess.
Here I watch and wait decision of my case.
Chorus
Here he is! The smell of human blood
smiles to greet me. He has twined his hands
round the image of the goddess immortal.

He is seeking protection; he wishes to be
subject to *trial* for what his hands did . . .
But that may *not* be! His mother's blood
has fallen to earth; it cannot be recalled.
It was shed and spread on the ground and is gone.

(To Orestes.)

But blood to match blood
you must give me to gulp from your living self,
rich blood-cake from your limbs.
Living as you are, I will waste you,
and haul you beneath the earth,
that you may pay for your mother's agony
with pains that shall match hers.
Write it down in the tablets of your mind.

Orestes

    The blood is falling asleep; it is melting off my hand,
and the taint of mother-killing has washed away.
Yes, it *was* fresh once, and at the hearth
of Phoebus Apollo
it was expelled by pig sacrifices.
Time, aging, pulls down everything alike.
So now with holy lips I call, in reverence,
Athena, queen of this land, to come and help me.
May she come to me to deliver me from evil.

Chorus

    No, neither Apollo, nor Athena's strength
will rescue you. Answer me now! Do you despise my words?
You, raised to be mine, a victim sacred to me!
You shall be my feast while still the life is in you,
the blood sucked from you, fodder for ghosts,
a shade. Against this man,
who keeps secret his murderous hands,
we are upright witnesses for those dead,
exacters of blood in revenge against him.

Mother who bore me, O Mother Night,
how we punish those in the dark
and those who still see, oh hear!
For Apollo has dishonored me,
has stolen this cowering hare of mine,
this thing that is truly sacred to me,
because of his mother's blood.
Over the one to be sacrificed
here is our hymn, driving mind askew,
wrenching it from its course,
working its mischief:

Orestes

This is the Furies' song,
chains on the mind, no sound of the lyre,
it wastes away mortal men.

Chorus

Mortal men who whose lot was to do
the wanton murder of their own kin—
we shall attend these until
they enter the clay of earth;
and dead, too, shall not be free too much.
Over the one to be sacrificed
here is our hymn, driving mind askew,
wrenching it from its course,
working its mischief.

Orestes

This is the Furies' song,
chains on the mind, no sound of the lyre,
it wastes away mortal men.

Chorus

It all abides; we are the contrivers,
the perfecters of evil, keen-memoried,
holy, inaccessible to mortal prayers.
We follow a task dishonored,

a function quite separate from the gods',
under a light that knows no sun.

(*Enter Athena.*)

Athena

I have heard a cry from afar,
and here I see this company,
new to this land. And I but wonder;
I look and wonder. Who can they be? I speak
to all of you—to you, the stranger
who sat at my image, and to you there, who are
not like to anything begotten.

Chorus

Daughter of Zeus, you shall know all, and quickly,
for we are Night's dark children; we are called
the Curses in our places under the earth.

Athena

I know your race and know your titles, too.

Chorus

We drive from their houses those that murdered others.

Athena

What is the limit of this hunt for the killer?

Chorus

Where joy can never more be part of life.

Athena

Is this the hunt you set upon this man?

Chorus

Yes; he confessed he was his mother's killer.

Athena

Was he not subject to the force of another's anger?

Chorus

What is the force that drives to matricide?

Athena

This is one half of the case; there are two sides.

Chorus

Then, try the case, you; give a straight judgment.

Athena

Will the settlement of the case, then, rest with *me?*

Chorus

Why not? We find you worthy.

Athena

What have you to say, in turn, stranger, to this?
Tell us your country and your family
and your circumstances; and then fight the case
against their slander of you.

Orestes

O Queen Athena:
I am an Argive; and my father's name—
I am glad you ask it—it is Agamemnon,
the supreme marshal of our forces at sea.
With him you yourself rendered cityless that city
of Ilium, Troy. But he, my father, died,
shamefully, when he came to his own house. My mother
killed him, with cunning nets.
I myself was in exile before this, but I returned
and killed my mother,
killing to quit the killing of my dear father.
Apollo bore his share of the guilt for all of this with me,
for to spur me on, he threatened agonies
if I should not act against the guilty murderers.
Whether I did so justly or unjustly,
is now for you to judge.
However I fare, I am in your hands, content.

Athena

You have approached my house,
a suppliant purified and harmless.
But *these* have functions not lightly to be dismissed,
and if the judgment does not go their way,
afterward the poison that drips from their minds
will fall to the ground and be a pestilence
deadly and dark.
So the matter stands.

The outcome for both sides
contains helpless disaster.
This is too great an issue for men
to pronounce judgment on,
nor is it in accordance with sacred law
that I should decide the issue of murder.
But since the case has fallen to me,
I will choose judges with respect for an oath
and so set up an ordinance for ever.

Chorus

Here now is an outcome
of the new institutions,
if the plea and the crime
of the mother-killer shall prevail.
For, immediately, this act shall fit
all men for easiness of hand.
For there await parents, in days to come,
many a wounding stroke dealt
by their truly begotten children.
For there will be no brooding wrath
of the Furies, that watch mankind,
to attend upon such deeds.
There is a place where terror is good;
it should sit and watch over the mind.
Wisdom comes through
the cramping of limits.
Where there is a man who in light of day
fears nothing in his heart;
where there is a city of such men—which men, what city
fears justice as once they did?
Do not praise
the life anarchic
nor the life ruled by a master.
God has granted

the supremacy in everything
to the mean
between the two.
The word I speak is a balanced word.
Chorus
My Lord Apollo, rule where rule is yours.
What have you to do with this?
Apollo
I have come to give my witness;
this man in all due usage
is my suppliant, and I have purified him of murder.
So I will be his advocate—for I, too, bear the blame
for this man's mother's murder.

(*Speaking to Athena.*)

Introduce the case and judge it,
according to your knowledge.
Athena (*to the Furies*)
It is for you to make your speech.
I declare the proceedings open.
The prosecutor should speak first; that way
he may properly inform us of the matter.
Chorus (*to Orestes*)
First, declare whether you *did* kill your mother.
Orestes
Yes, I killed her. I do not deny that.
Chorus
There is one of the three wrestling falls already.
Orestes
I am not yet on the ground for you to boast over me.
Chorus
Very well; then tell us how you killed her.
Orestes
With sword in hand I cut her throat.
Chorus
At whose incentive and by whose plans?

Orestes

By Apollo's oracles; he is here, my witness.

Chorus

The prophet instructed you to kill your mother?

Orestes

Yes, and so far I do not fault what has happened.

Chorus

You will, however, if the vote condemns you.

Orestes

I have my trust; from the grave my father will help me.

Chorus

You trust the dead—when you have killed your mother!

Orestes

Yes, for she was stained with double blood-guiltiness.

Chorus

How was that? Inform your judges here.

Orestes

She killed, in the same man,
her husband and my father.

Chorus

But you are alive—and she now quit of the murder!

Orestes

Why did you not hunt *her* to banishment
when she was alive?

Chorus

Because she was no blood kin to him she killed.

Orestes

I am blood kin, then, to my mother?

Chorus

How else did she raise you in her womb, her murderer?
Your dearest blood tie, to your mother, do you disown it?

Orestes

Apollo, new bear witness, now expose
how I have killed her justly.

Apollo

I will speak to *you* (*he motions to the whole assembly*),

this great court of Athens.
I will speak justly, for I am a prophet and will not lie.
Upon my prophet's throne
I never yet spoke of man or woman or city
a word that was not bidden me by Zeus,
father of the Olympians. Be advised
how strong that justice is; I bid you follow his will.
There is no oath stronger than Zeus.

Chorus

Zeus, you say, Zeus gave you this oracle
to tell Orestes here that in avenging
his father's murder he should forever dishonor his mother!

Apollo

It is not the same for a nobleman to die—
honored with the scepter, which the gods give princes—
as to die by a woman's hand, not with furious arrows
launched by an Amazon, from afar, but, as you will hear.
He had come from war; he was received with loyalty;
then as he went through his bath she enfolded him,
at the end, with a robe, and had him fettered.
In those embroidered folds, she struck him down.
This was the end of majesty and the great fleet's commander.

Chorus

According to your story, Zeus gives precedence
to the fate of a father; but he himself
fettered his father.
I call the judges to witness, to hear this.

Apollo

You loathsome creatures, hated by the gods,
one may break *fetters*.
But when the dust has snatched to itself the blood
of a man once dead, there is no resurrection.

Chorus

Look to how you defend acquittal of this man.
He has shed on the ground his mother's blood—

will he then live in his father's house in Argos?
What public altars will he use?
Apollo
   This I will tell you; mark how clear my words.
   She that is called the mother of the child
   is not its parent, but the nurse of the new seed;
   it is the stallion's thrust that is the parent;
   the woman saves the young living plant for a stranger,
   as she is a stranger to him.
   I will give you proof of what I say; a father
   may generate without a mother; see—
   here is at hand my witness—the child of Olympian Zeus.
   She never lay in the womb's dark recesses;
   she is a living plant, such as no goddess could bear.
Athena
   I now bid the judges in all honesty
   give a true judgment.
Chorus
   I remain to hear how the decision shall be made.
Apollo
   You have heard what you have heard;
   in the truth of your hearts, give your votes—
   and respect the oaths you have sworn.
Athena
   You who judge this first trial of bloodshed.
   This shall be for all time to come for the people of Athens
   the judges' council chamber. For this is Ares' hill,
   and this the Areopagus.
   Here is the city's Reverence. And her brother, Fear,
   shall, among the citizens, check injustice
   night and day alike.
   Do not cast terror utterly
   out of your city; for what man is just
   that has no fear of anything? If the citizens
   fear what they honor, justly, they shall have

a saving fortress in their land and city,
such as no other people of mankind possess.
This shall be a council chamber untouched by gain,
revered, a true guard over your land,
watchful for those who sleep.
Now, be upright, and with reverence for your oath
bear your vote and decide the case.

(*They cast their votes.*)

Chorus

I shall give you counsel; do not dishonor
this company of ours; we can be dangerous.

Apollo

And I bid you fear those oracles
that are both mine and Zeus's; let them not be fruitless.

Chorus (to Apollo)

Bloodshed is not your function,
but you honor it.
Henceforth the oracles you give will be impure.
If I lose the case,
I will be a danger to this land henceforth.

Apollo

Neither among the gods that are new or old
do you find honor. I shall win over you.

Chorus

You have ridden me down, young god as I am old.
I wait to hear the settlement.

Athena

Let the judges now proceed
to cast out the votes from the urns that contain them.

Chorus

O Night, dark Mother, are you watching?

Orestes

For me it is death, or the light of life.

Chorus

For us, destruction or continued honor.

(*Silence.*)

Athena
 The vote is equal and the judgment mine.
 The man has been acquitted in the murder suit.
Orestes
 Pallas Athena, you have saved my house.
 I that had lost a fatherland am restored to my house
 by you. Truly, some Greek will say,
 "There is an Argive who once again is home
 in all his father owned, thanks to *them,*
 Athena and Apollo and the Savior who rules all."
 Now I shall go to my home again, in peace.
Chorus
 O you young gods, you have ridden down
 the old ways; you have snatched them out of my hands.
 I have no more honor, but in my wretchedness
 my anger will be heavy; on this land
 I will relieve my heart's pain, drops on the earth,
 poison, overbearing poison.
 A blight will come of it—no leaves, no children—
 O Justice! The blight will attack the land
 and cast upon it infections which kill its people.
 O great unlucky daughters of Night,
 dishonored in your sorrow.
Athena
 You have not been conquered—
 the suit has truly ended
 with equal votes; you have no dishonor in that.
 But there was the clearest testimony from Zeus—
 he gave the oracles
 that Orestes should come to no harm from his act.
 Will *you* then vomit your dark hate against
 this land? Reflect; do not rage so, do not
 bring infertility upon the land. For I
 make an absolute promise to you, in all justice,
 that within this country you may sit at the hearth

on gleaming thrones, and be honored
by all the citizens.

Chorus

O you young gods, you have ridden down
the old ways.
A blight will come of it—no leaves, no children—
Justice!

Athena

Lull to sleep the bitter strength of the dark blood;
for you can share my majesty and peace.

Chorus

That I should suffer so!
I with my thoughts of ancient times,
that I should dwell beneath the earth.
Hear me, Mother Night.
For the ancient honors of the gods
have been snatched away and made nothing of.

Athena

If you find sacred the honor of Persuasion,
the sweetness of my tongue, its power to charm,
then remain here with us; for you may certainly
be our land's lord, justly honored for ever.

Chorus

Lady Athena, what is the home you speak of?

Athena

One free of all unhappiness; only receive the gift.

Chorus

And if I do? What honor continues mine?

Athena

No household will thrive without you.

Chorus

Will you indeed allow me so much power?

Athena

I shall.

Chorus

And you will guarantee this for all time?

Athena

    I do not promise what I will not perform.

Chorus

    I give over my anger.

    I shall not dishonor the city.

    I pray that the sun's bright radiance

    bring from the earth abundantly

    all goods of life that depend on Fortune.

Athena

    I praise you for the meanings of your prayers.

    I shall send you on your way with light

    of radiant torches to those places

    underneath, beneath our earth.

    Advance, in order, great and venerable,

    you virgin daughters of Night.

    Holy silence. Beneath the ancient caverns of the earth,

    be glorified, in honor, in sacrifice, and in Fortune.

    Holy silence.